NEW DIRECTIONS FOR INSTITUTIONAL RESEARCH

J. Fredericks Volkwein, *Penn State University*
EDITOR-IN-CHIEF

Larry H. Litten, *Dartmouth College*
ASSOCIATE EDITOR

The Student Ratings Debate: Are They Valid? How Can We Best Use Them?

Michael Theall
University of Illinois

Philip C. Abrami
Concordia University

Lisa A. Mets
Eckerd College

EDITORS

D1462441

Number 109, Spring 2001

JOSSEY-BASS
San Francisco

THE STUDENT RATINGS DEBATE: ARE THEY VALID? HOW CAN WE BEST USE THEM?
Michael Theall, Philip C. Abrami, Lisa A. Mets, (eds.)
New Directions for Institutional Research, no. 109
Volume XXVII, Number 5
J. Fredericks Volkwein, Editor-in-Chief

New Directions for Institutional Research is indexed in *College Student Personnel Abstracts, Contents Pages in Education,* and *Current Index to Journals in Education* (ERIC).

Microfilm copies of issues and chapters are available in 16mm and 35mm, as well as microfiche in 105mm, through University Microfilms Inc., 300 North Zeeb Road, Ann Arbor, Michigan 48106-1346.

ISSN 0271-0579   ISBN 0-7879-5756-9

NEW DIRECTIONS FOR INSTITUTIONAL RESEARCH is part of The Jossey-Bass Higher and Adult Education Series and is published quarterly by Jossey-Bass, 350 Sansome Street, San Francisco, California 94104-1342 (publication number USPS 098-830). Periodicals postage paid at San Francisco, California, and at additional mailing offices. POSTMASTER: Send address changes to New Directions for Institutional Research, Jossey-Bass Inc., Publishers, 350 Sansome Street, San Francisco, California 94104-1342.

SUBSCRIPTIONS cost $59.00 for individuals and $109.00 for institutions, agencies, and libraries.

EDITORIAL CORRESPONDENCE should be sent to J. Fredericks Volkwein, Center for the Study of Higher Education, Penn State University, 403 South Allen Street, Suite 104, University Park, PA 16801-5252.

Photograph of the library by Michael Graves at San Juan Capistrano by Chad Slattery © 1984. All rights reserved.

www.josseybass.com

Printed in the United States of America on acid-free recycled paper containing 100 percent recovered waste paper, of which at least 20 percent is postconsumer waste.

THE ASSOCIATION FOR INSTITUTIONAL RESEARCH was created in 1966 to benefit, assist, and advance research leading to improved understanding, planning,
and operation of institutions of higher education. Publication policy is set by
its Publications Committee.

For information about the Association for Institutional Research, write to the
following address:

AIR Executive Office
114 Stone Building
Florida State University
Tallahassee, FL 32306-4462

(850) 644-4470

air@mailer.fsu.edu
http://airweb.org

Contents

Editors' Notes

This volume of *New Directions for Institutional Research* is devoted to student ratings, a topic that continues to occupy a central role in postsecondary education. Student ratings of instruction are also called teacher rating forms (TRFs), techer course evaluations (TCEs), student ratings of teaching effectiveness (SRTEs), or student evaluations of teaching (SETs). They are widely used on college and university campuses in North America and increasingly throughout the world as sources of feedback on instructional effectiveness. They serve as tools for instructional improvement, as evidence for promotion and tenure decisions, as the means for student course selection, as one criterion of program effectiveness, and as the continuing focus of active research and intensive debate.

Student ratings of instruction are often provided on a multi-item questionnaire that contains as many as three dozen questions about the instructor and the course in which students are enrolled. These may be questions about the overall effectiveness of the instructor or the course (for example, "How would you rate the instructor's all-around teaching ability?" "How much did you learn in this course relative to other courses you have taken?"). They may be about specific aspects of the course and about specific aspects of teaching ("Did the instructor synthesize ideas?" "Was the instructor friendly?"). In addition, students are often asked to complete open-ended items providing an opportunity for them to express more detailed thoughts and feelings about the course, the instructor, and their learning.

Summary of the Contents

The present volume offers a summary of key issues surrounding student ratings and some provocative suggestions for new directions for research and practice. You will find that it effectively blends the new with the old and provides an insightful and refreshing approach to this important subject.

The chapters in Part One summarize the research evidence and the controversies surrounding student ratings of instruction. The consistency of the experts' judgment reinforces the clarity of the conclusions that can be drawn. Yet their different emphases should prove useful to both research and practice.

In Chapter One, James A. Kulik reviews the conclusions on which most experts agree, based on the voluminous research on student ratings. He cites some of the main sources of these conclusions. He also discusses some dissenting opinions and the research support for these opinions.

He begins by focusing on the validity of student ratings and four of the most credible of the indicators of instructional effectiveness: student learning, student comments, alumni ratings, and observer ratings. He concludes that rating results agree well, but not perfectly, with results from each of these indicators.

Kulik next examines the utility of student ratings. Research studies indicate that feedback from ratings, especially when coupled with expert consultation, helps faculty improve their teaching. He also points out, however, that very little evidence exists on the effects of rating programs on instruction at the institutional level.

Finally, Kulik considers several areas of recent controversy: Do high ratings imply low learning? Does showmanship or body language affect ratings? Do ratings reflect lenient grading? Does vocal expressiveness influence ratings? Kulik notes that the studies that have drawn the attention of critics of student ratings contain fairly serious methodological flaws, seemingly justifying challenges to their findings. Nevertheless, he calls for follow-up research on the issues they raise so that we can judge how dependable the findings are.

In Chapter Two, John C. Ory and Katherine Ryan review the evidence on the construct validity of student ratings both from the established perspective and from the new perspective as summarized in the latest standards on educational and psychological testing. They also remind us that validity is not a property of a test but a characteristic of the meaning and interpretation of the test scores and any actions based on those scores.

From the established perspective, they look at five types of ratings research: multisection, multitrait-multimethod, bias, laboratory, and dimensional. Their brief summaries of the evidence from the traditional perspective are consistent with the conclusions reached by Kulik.

Ory and Ryan go on to examine how well the evidence addresses questions raised within the new perspective on validity. Is there a relationship between the content of the student ratings form and the construct intended to be measured? Does the nature of the student rating process fit the construct being measured? To what extent do the relationships among test items and test components correspond to the construct domain? Is there a relationship between student ratings and variables external to the ratings that are expected to be predicted by the ratings and similar measures of the intended construct? Would the relationship, or lack thereof, found between student ratings and various external variables exist in different settings with different students at different times? How does the evidence of the intended and unintended consequences of testing inform validity decisions and our use of the tests? This last question is given special consideration.

In Chapter Three, Michael Theall and Jennifer Franklin present a third review of the literature on student ratings, but they begin by examining the controversy surrounding student ratings as rooted in poor summative practice and in the psychology—self-efficacy, casual attributions, and personal expectancies—of faculty whose careers may be affected by rating results.

They also consider ratings myths and ratings evidence. Are students qualified to rate their instructors and the instruction they receive? Are ratings based solely on popularity? Are ratings related to learning? Can students make accurate judgments while still in class or in school? Are student ratings reliable? Does gender make a difference? Are ratings affected by situational variables? Do students rate teachers on the basis of expected or given grades?

Importantly, Theall and Franklin go on to recommend a set of guidelines for good evaluation practice: establish the purpose of the evaluation and the uses and users of ratings beforehand; include all stakeholders in decisions about the evaluation criteria, process, and procedures; publicly present clear information about the evaluation criteria, process, and procedures; produce reports that can be easily and accurately understood; educate the users of rating results to avoid misuses and misinterpretation; keep a balance between individual and institutional needs in mind; include resources for improvement and support of teaching and teachers; keep formative evaluation confidential and separate from summative evaluation; adhere to rigorous psychometric and measurement principles and practice; regularly evaluate the evaluation system; establish legally defensible processes and a system for grievances; and consider the appropriate combination of evaluative data with assessment and institutional research information.

The chapters in Part Two are more methodological in focus. They deal with ways to improve the quality of information that may be extracted from ratings.

These chapters are closely linked. Chapter Four, by Philip C. Abrami, grew out of the 1998 W. J. McKeachie Award Invited Address delivered at the annual meeting of the American Educational Research Association. Abrami spoke of a mathematical means by which to facilitate the correct summative decisions about instructor effectiveness based on student ratings. Because his ideas were controversial, an arrangement was made to use the Web site and electronic distribution list of the Special Interest Group in Faculty Teaching Evaluation and Development (SIGFTED) to solicit comments and reactions. The comments and replies were both reasonably extensive and extremely thoughtful. They are summarized in Chapter Five by Michael Theall, with Abrami reserving the last word—for now—in his rejoinder in Chapter Six.

What Lies Ahead and Beyond

No single volume can ever be complete, especially one that addresses such a voluminous and dynamic literature, such an important topic, and such a wide-ranging set of controversies. Because of this, we thought we would take some space to reflect on a few things that this volume does not cover.

First, the philosophies and approaches to postsecondary instruction are undergoing major change. Traditional didactic forms of instruction are being replaced by more learner-centered approaches.

In 1997, the American Psychological Association's Board of Educational Affairs distributed a list of fourteen learner-centered principles, intended as a framework for educational reform and redesign (see Exhibit I.1). These principles pertain to both the learner and the learning process and focus on psychological factors under the learner's internal control rather than on conditioned habits or physiological factors. They are intended to deal holistically with learners in the context of real-world learning situations.

Exhibit I.1. Fourteen Learner-Centered Principles

Cognitive and Metacognitive Factors

1. *Nature of the learning process.* The learning of complex subject matter is most effective when it is an intentional process of constructing meaning from information and experience.
2. *Goals of the learning process.* The successful learner, over time and with support and instructional guidance, can create meaningful, coherent representations of knowledge.
3. *Construction of knowledge.* The successful learner can link new information with existing knowledge in meaningful ways.
4. *Strategic thinking.* The successful learner can create and use a repertoire of thinking and reasoning strategies to achieve complex learning goals.
5. *Thinking about thinking.* Higher order strategies for selecting and monitoring mental operations facilitate creative and critical thinking.
6. *Context of learning.* Learning is influenced by environmental factors, including culture, technology, and instructional practices.

Motivational and Affective Factors

7. *Motivational and emotional influences on learning.* What and how much is learned is influenced by the learner's motivation. Motivation to learn, in turn, is influenced by the individual's emotional states, beliefs, interests and goals, and habits of thinking.
8. *Intrinsic motivation to learn.* The learner's creativity, higher order thinking, and natural curiosity all contribute to motivation to learn. Intrinsic motivation is stimulated by tasks of optimal novelty and difficulty, relevant to personal interests, and providing for personal choice and control.
9. *Effects of motivation on effort.* Acquisition of complex knowledge and skills requires extended learner effort and guided practice. Without learners' motivation to learn, the willingness to exert this effort is unlikely without coercion.

Developmental and Social Factors

10. *Developmental influences on learning.* As individuals develop, there are different opportunities and constraints for learning. Learning is most effective when differential development within and across physical, intellectual, emotional, and social domains is taken into account.
11. *Social influences on learning.* Learning is influenced by social interactions, interpersonal relations, and communication with others.

Individual Differences

12. *Individual differences in learning.* Learners have different strategies, approaches, and capabilities for learning that are a function of prior experience and heredity.
13. *Learning and diversity.* Learning is most effective when differences in learners' linguistic, cultural, and social backgrounds are taken into account.
14. *Standards and assessment.* Setting appropriately high and challenging standards and assessing the learner as well as learning progress—including diagnostic, process, and outcome assessment—are integral parts of the learning process.

Source: Adapted from American Psychological Association, 1997.

We may need to redesign student rating instruments to reflect these learner-centered approaches to instruction. For example, we may wish to include items that assess such things as whether the instructor facilitated positive interdependence and individual accountability when using cooperative and collaborative learning techniques. We may also ask about how well instructors facilitate problem-based inquiry. Finally, in student-centered classrooms, we may also be more concerned with whether and how students engage in self-regulated learning.

A second area of concern is the use of technology for learning both as a way to supplement traditional instruction and as a means to deliver instruction at a distance. Both enthusiasm for technology for learning and apprehension regarding its use appear to be widespread as we move more deeply into the information age. Will the personal computer be as indispensable a tool for learning as Guttenburg's printing press, or will it become another passing educational fad like televised instruction? Some analysts are convinced that computer technology can be a powerful and flexible tool for learning. Indeed, there is sufficient optimism in technology's potential to have a positive impact on learning that government agencies around the world have established committees to advise them and postsecondary institutions on the best ways to deliver on-line learning. There is also, however, sufficient skepticism that distance education and the general trend toward the virtual university are problematic and may even represent serious threats to higher education.

Procedures and approaches for the wise integration of technology for learning are in their infancy. Tools to evaluate them must be adapted from what currently exists. New research will be needed not only to tell us what to evaluate but also to determine whether new tools will lead us to superior ways to visually represent and dynamically interpret information on teaching and instruction.

Philip C. Abrami
Michael Theall
Lisa A. Mets
Editors

Reference

American Psychological Association."Learner-Centered Psychological Principles: A Framework for School Reform and Redesign." [http://www.apa.org/ed/lcp2/homepage.html]. 1997.

PHILIP C. ABRAMI *is professor and director of the Centre for the Study of Learning and Performance at Concordia University, Montreal, Quebec, Canada.*

MICHAEL THEALL *is associate professor of educational administration and director of the Center for Teaching and Learning at the University of Illinois at Springfield.*

LISA A. METS *is executive assistant to the president at Eckerd College, St. Petersburg, Florida.*

PART ONE

Summarizing the Evidence

1

*This chapter reviews the conclusions on which most
experts agree, cites some of the main sources of support
for these conclusions, and discusses some dissenting
opinions and the research support for those opinions.*

Student Ratings: Validity, Utility, and Controversy

James A. Kulik

Student ratings are an old topic in higher education. Seventy-five years have
passed since students at the University of Washington filled out what were
arguably the first student rating forms (Guthrie, 1954). Almost as long a time
has passed since researchers at Purdue University published the first research
studies on student ratings (Remmers and Brandenburg, 1927). But student
ratings are not yet a stale topic. Teachers still talk about them, researchers still
study them, and most important, students still fill out the forms—millions of
them every year—in college classes throughout the country.

Seldin's surveys on teaching evaluation (1993a) show just how widespread rating systems have become. About 29 percent of American colleges
reported using student ratings to evaluate teaching in Seldin's 1973 survey,
68 percent of colleges reported using them in his 1983 survey, and 86 percent reported using them in his 1993 survey. Seldin reported that no other
data source gets more attention in the evaluation of teaching—not classroom visits, not examination scores, and not self-reports.

Rating results are also being used today in more ways than ever before.
Colleges originally set up rating systems to serve two purposes: to help
administrators monitor teaching quality and to help teachers improve their
teaching (Guthrie, 1954). Today, ratings serve many purposes. At my own
institution, administrators and administrative committees use ratings in hiring new faculty, in annual reviews of current faculty, in promotion and tenure
decisions, in school accreditation reviews, in selecting faculty and graduate
students for teaching awards and honors, and in assigning teachers to
courses. Faculty members use ratings when trying to improve their teaching
effectiveness, in documenting their effectiveness internally and externally,

and in monitoring the performance of their graduate student assistants. Graduate student instructors use ratings in developing their teaching skills and in documenting these skills in job applications. Student groups use the ratings in selecting courses and in selecting teachers for awards and honors.

Many teachers applaud the increased use of ratings on college campuses. They view ratings as reliable and valid measures that bring scientific accuracy to the evaluation of teaching, and they also argue that ratings give students more of a voice in their education. But not everyone is so enthusiastic. Some teachers view ratings as meaningless quantification. They fear that students too often use the power of their pencils to get even with professors and warn that rating systems may turn the evaluation of effective teaching into a personality contest.

Researchers have collected a wealth of data on student ratings over the years. One might suppose that the research studies on ratings are similar to many other studies in education: conflicting, confusing, and inconclusive. And some of the studies of ratings are. It is a mistake, however, to ignore this research literature.

In this chapter, I review the conclusions on which most experts agree. I cite some of the main sources of support for these conclusions, and I discuss some dissenting opinions and the research support for those opinions.

Validity of Student Ratings

To say that student ratings are valid is to say that they reflect teaching effectiveness. It would therefore seem to be a straightforward matter to assess the validity of student ratings. All we have to do is to correlate student ratings with teaching effectiveness scores. If ratings are valid, students will give good ratings to effective teachers and poor ratings to ineffective ones. The size of the correlation between ratings and effectiveness will provide a precise index of the validity of student ratings.

The catch is that no one knows what measure to use as *the* criterion of teaching effectiveness. Researchers have long searched for the perfect criterion. Among the criteria that they have examined are measures of student learning, alumni judgments of teachers, and classroom observations by experts. But the search has proved futile because each of these criteria is far from perfect.

Scriven (1983) is especially clear about the shortcomings of these measures. About learning measures, he has written, "The best teaching is not that which produces the most learning" (p. 248). According to Scriven, good examination performance may result from a number of factors besides good teaching. For example, a teacher may put so much pressure on students that they abandon their work in other classes. Such pressure tactics may produce good examination scores in the teacher's course, but the students pay too high a price for their accomplishments. The occasional use of such tactics by college teachers illustrates the general point that good examination performance can result from unethical or bad teaching. On a more practical note, the tests that teachers administer are often far from perfect. They are sometimes neither reliable nor valid measures of what is learned in class. They are usually an inadequate indicator of the influence that great teachers have on students' lives.

Scriven (1983) is equally clear about the weaknesses in expert visits to a classroom. Using such visits to evaluate teaching, he says, "is not just incorrect, it is a disgrace" (p. 251). The visits themselves alter teaching, Scriven points out, and the number of experts and visits is usually too small to yield a reliable measure of teaching effects. Furthermore, the experts who provide the ratings usually have biases that can skew their observations. Finally, classroom talk, which is the thing that the experts observe, is only a small part of what constitutes college teaching. Many things not observable in classroom discourse are necessary for good teaching, including fair grades and valid tests.

Scriven (1983) warns that alumni surveys are "essentially useless for evaluation of teachers" (p. 254). They usually have extremely low response rates and relate to "ancestors" of current performance. Alumni perspectives are sometimes dated—teachers change and times change—and alumni views about what will be valuable for a new generation of graduates may be wrong. Scriven concedes, however, "These reasons do not exclude some use of alumni surveys in selecting Distinguished (Elderly) Teacher Awards" (p. 254).

Not all experts on ratings are as passionate about the shortcomings of these measures as Scriven is. But all experts agree with him on the practical impossibility of finding a single perfect criterion of teaching effectiveness. With such a measure, we could calculate a predictive validity coefficient for student ratings. The correlation coefficient between ratings and effectiveness would give the degree to which we could predict effectiveness from ratings. Without a perfect criterion, it is impossible to reduce the validity of student ratings to a single number.

Given this difficulty, most researchers on ratings have adopted what is sometimes called a "construct validation approach" to student ratings. This approach requires researchers to show that ratings correlate to a satisfactory degree with other admittedly partial and imperfect measures of effectiveness. Experts do not expect perfect agreement between ratings and such imperfect measures, but they do expect student ratings to correlate at least moderately with these other measures.

In this section, I focus on the agreement between ratings and four of the most credible of the indicators of effectiveness: student learning, student comments, alumni ratings, and ratings of teaching by outside observers. I conclude that rating results agree adequately, but not perfectly, with results from each of these indicators. Teachers who come out high on one measure usually come out high on other measures, too.

Students Learn More from Highly Rated Teachers. The best data on the correlation between ratings and learning come from dozens of studies of student ratings in multisection college courses. In these studies, instructors teach a section of a course in their own way, but all instructors cover the same content and administer the same common final examination. To determine whether superior ratings go with better or poorer exam performance, researchers correlate section averages on the examination with section averages on the rating scales. Researchers conducting such studies have usually found that examination and rating averages correlate positively. They have concluded therefore that students generally give high ratings to teachers from whom they learn most, and they generally give low ratings to teachers from whom they learn least.

Some of the many reviews are narrative in form (Costin, Greenough, and Menges, 1971; Kulik and McKeachie, 1975). Others are meta-analytic reports (Cohen, 1981, 1982; Feldman, 1989c; McCallum, 1984). The meta-analytic reviews are clearer than the narrative ones, and the clearest of the meta-analyses, Peter Cohen's classic report (1981), which was the first one published.

Cohen's meta-analysis covered data from forty-one studies that reported on sixty-eight separate multisection courses. Like other meta-analysts, Cohen located his studies in objective computer searches of library databases. He then expressed the outcomes of all studies in terms of product-moment correlation coefficients, and he also coded the features of the studies in quantitative or quasi-quantitative terms. Finally, Cohen calculated the average result in all studies and in various subgroups of the studies.

Cohen found a strong relationship between student ratings and student learning in the average study. The average correlation of examination score with overall rating of the teacher was .43. The average correlation of examination score with an overall rating of the course was .47. Although there is no definite standard for interpreting size of correlation, Jacob Cohen (1977) has provided some rough guidelines stating that a coefficient of about .50 is large, a coefficient of about .30 is moderate, and a correlation of about .10 is small. According to these standards, the correlation between learning and an overall rating of the teacher or the course is moderate to high.

Although the average correlation between ratings and achievement measures was moderate to high in Cohen's analysis, he observed that not all studies produced the same results. Indeed, study results varied a great deal. Some studies reported a high positive correlation between ratings and achievement; other studies reported a negative correlation. Cohen was interested in finding some factor that might explain the variation in study findings. He examined twenty study features in his attempt to explain the variation.

He found, first of all, that the items included on a rating scale could influence study findings. The correlation between ratings and achievement was high for items involving instructor skill and for those measuring teacher and course organization. Correlation coefficients were moderate for items on teacher rapport and feedback near zero for items dealing with course difficulty.

A few other study features seemed to influence the findings. Specifically, correlation coefficients were higher in studies in which the instructors were full-time teachers, in studies in which students knew their final grade when they rated the instructor, and in studies where achievement tests were evaluated by an external evaluator. Cohen also reported that many other study characteristics (such as random assignment, course content, and availability of pretest data) were not significantly related to study findings.

Student Ratings Agree with Student Comments. Researchers have carried out only a few studies on the agreement between student ratings and the comments that students freely make about their teachers. The findings of the available studies are so clear, however, that they are worth noting (Braskamp, Ory, and Pieper, 1981; Ory, Braskamp, and Pieper, 1980). The evidence shows that ratings correlate strongly with comments that students make about their teachers both on questionnaires and in special interviews.

The most direct evidence for this point comes from Ory, Braskamp, and Pieper's study of comments and ratings (1980). These authors focused on classes in which students filled out rating forms, wrote answers to open-ended questions about the course and teacher, and spoke to consultants about the course in group interviews. The students made their ratings on 6-point scales, and the researchers coded the students' written and interview comments on the same scales. Finally, the researchers correlated the data from the three sources.

Ory and his colleagues found a remarkable degree of consistency between student ratings and the ratings of a class derived from written and interview comments. Student ratings of the course and instructor correlated .94 and .93 with ratings derived from written comments; student ratings of the course and instructor correlated .81 and .84 with ratings derived from student comments in interviews. Along with Ory and his colleagues, I conclude from this study that the extraordinarily high correlation between comments and ratings suggests that these data sources give nearly identical pictures of teaching effectiveness.

Student Ratings Agree with Observer Ratings. Murray (1983) carried out an especially careful study of the relationship between student ratings and ratings of teaching behaviors made by trained observers. He arranged for forty-nine students in an educational psychology course to report on the teaching behaviors of fifty-four college teachers. From student ratings made in an earlier semester, these teachers could be classified as high, medium, or low in effectiveness. Six to eight of the observers rated each of the fifty-four teachers in three separate one-hour class periods; the observers thus spent a total of eighteen to twenty-four hours with each teacher. During the three-month observation period, the observers saw clear differences in the teaching behavior of the three groups. In all, the three groups differed on twenty-six individual behaviors. The sharpest differences were in behaviors indicating teacher clarity, enthusiasm, and rapport. Highly rated teachers were high and low-rated teachers were low in these three qualities.

Feldman (1989c) reviewed findings from Murray's study and four other studies that correlated student ratings with ratings made by outside observers. The average correlation coefficient between student ratings and observer ratings in these studies was .50. By conventional standards, this is a high correlation. It is especially impressive when we consider that outside observers and students do not have access to the same data. For example, observers are usually not aware of teacher behavior outside the classroom. They usually know little or nothing about the quality of teacher comments to students on their written work, the teacher's fairness in grading students, or the teacher's availability to students outside of class.

The essential point is that students give favorable ratings to teachers who get good marks from outside observers, and they give unfavorable ratings to teachers who get poor marks. Thus student ratings correlate highly with ratings by outside observers.

Student Ratings Agree with Alumni Ratings. The best evidence of agreement between student and alumni ratings of teachers comes from a longitudinal study by Overall and Marsh (1980). The fourteen hundred students in this study filled out end-of-term evaluation forms in all the courses they took during a three-year period. One year after the students graduated and one to four years after the students completed these courses, the students again filled out evaluation forms on their courses. The end-of-term ratings in one hundred courses correlated .83 with the follow-up ratings, and the median rating at the two times was nearly identical.

Additional support for the stability of ratings comes from cross-sectional studies. In these studies, different cohorts of students provide the current-student and alumni ratings. The cross-sectional design is weaker than a longitudinal design because the different cohorts of students base their ratings on different experiences with a teacher. Feldman (1989c) reviewed results from six cross-sectional studies. He found an average correlation coefficient of .69 between current-student and alumni ratings. By Jacob Cohen's standards (1977), this is a remarkably high correlation.

Thus current students and alumni give similar ratings to teachers. The findings do not support the argument that students can evaluate their courses only after they have been asked to apply course material in further courses or in their postgraduation pursuits. Instead, current students give favorable ratings to teachers whom alumni remember fondly and poor marks to teachers whom alumni remember unfavorably.

The central point that emerges from research studies and reviews on validity of ratings is that teachers who receive high ratings from their students receive high marks on other credible criteria of teaching effectiveness. Students give high ratings to the teachers from whom they learn most. They also comment favorably about these teachers in writing and in interviews. In addition, outside observers give highly rated teachers excellent ratings, and alumni ratings of the teachers are excellent. Researchers have studied the agreement of student ratings and several other possible measures of teaching effectiveness, including self-ratings and ratings made by departmental colleagues who have not visited the teacher's classroom (Feldman, 1989c). I consider these to be less satisfactory measures of teaching effectiveness, and so I have not reviewed findings on such measures here. It is worth noting, however, that student ratings agree well with these measures too.

Utility of Student Ratings

Student rating programs are meant to improve college teaching in at least two ways. First, rating programs are meant to have effects at the institutional level. They may influence an institution's hiring decisions, merit increases, promotion and tenure decisions, and course assignments. Ratings may thus influence who teaches at a college, what courses they teach, and how much attention faculty members give to teaching. In addition, ratings are meant to have effects on individual teachers. Rating results give teachers information that they may use when trying to improve their own teaching.

Researchers have not yet developed a way of studying institutional effects of rating systems. They can point to the ubiquity of rating programs on college campuses or the longevity of many programs as presumptive evidence for the salutary effects of these programs, but hard data on institutional effects are scarce or nonexistent. Fortunately, researchers have paid far more attention to effects of student ratings on individual teachers. Researchers have carried out numerous studies on this topic, and reviewers agree on the main conclusions that can be drawn from the studies.

The basic design that researchers usually use to study rating effects on individual teachers is a two-group design. One group of teachers receives rating feedback in the middle of a course, and another group of teachers does not receive such feedback. At the end of the course, students again rate the teachers. To determine whether the midterm feedback from students is effective, the researcher compares the end-of-term ratings for the two groups.

Two studies carried out by Marsh and his colleagues (Marsh, Fleiner, and Thomas, 1975; Overall and Marsh, 1979) provide a good introduction to results in this area. In the first study, Marsh and his colleagues returned midterm student rating results to faculty and found that midterm feedback has a positive but modest effect. In the second study, the researchers met with instructors in the feedback group to discuss the evaluations and possible strategies for improvement. Not only did teachers in the feedback-plus-consultation group receive better end-of-term ratings from their students, but their students also performed better on the final examination.

Peter Cohen (1980) carried out a meta-analysis of findings in twenty-two studies of feedback effectiveness. His results parallel the results of the two studies by Marsh and colleagues. Cohen found that midterm feedback alone has a modest effect on end-of-term ratings. Such feedback raised end-of-term ratings by an average of about 0.1 rating point. Cohen also found that effects of midterm feedback are greater when instructors receive some consulting help along with the midterm ratings. End-of-term ratings went up by about 0.3 rating point in these circumstances.

The picture that emerges from the literature on utility of ratings is a hopeful one, but it has many blank areas. We know that rating programs have a long history in American higher education and that rating programs are ubiquitous on college campuses today. Rating programs thus seem to serve some useful purpose, but research on the effects of rating programs on colleges and universities is almost nonexistent. Much more research is available on the effect that ratings have on individual teachers. Research studies indicate that rating feedback helps teachers improve their teaching performance. The studies also suggest that student feedback is especially useful when rating results are coupled with consultation on improvement strategies.

Another View of Ratings

Analysts who question the validity and utility of student ratings seldom cite the evidence that I have reviewed. They are more likely to cite findings of a handful of well-known studies that are critical of ratings. These studies include Rodin and Rodin's study of student ratings and learning (1972), Naftulin, Ware, and Donnelly's study of "educational seduction" and ratings (1973), Ambady and Rosenthal's study of thin slices of expressive behavior and ratings (1992), Greenwald and Gillmore's study of grading, student work, and ratings (1997), and Williams and Ceci's study of expressiveness and ratings (1997). The studies suggest that instead of measuring teaching effectiveness, ratings reflect peripheral factors, such as teacher personality or grading standards.

I shall now briefly describe and comment on the five studies and their findings.

Do High Ratings Imply Low Learning? Rodin and Rodin (1972) reported a negative correlation of −.75 between student rating and student learning measures in an undergraduate calculus course. They concluded from this study that students rate most highly instructors from whom they learn least, and they rate least favorably instructors from whom they learn most. The Rodin and Rodin report on this research appeared in the prestigious and widely read journal *Science*. There it probably attracted more attention than any study of ratings ever had before. Critics of ratings still sometimes cite the Rodin and Rodin finding as evidence that student ratings lack validity.

Experts on ratings, however, have roundly criticized the study (for example, Doyle, 1975; Marsh, 1984). Critics point out that the ratings collected in the study were not of the course instructor but rather of the instructor's eleven teaching assistants. These teaching assistants actually played a minor role in course instruction. In addition, the learning measure was not a test given under standard conditions at the end of the course. Instead, Rodin and Rodin measured student learning by counting the number of examination problems that a student was able to solve during the term. The researchers gave students a total of forty examination problems, one after each course unit, and they allowed students who did not solve a problem on the first attempt to try again as many as six times without penalty. Furthermore, Rodin and Rodin had each teaching assistant score the problems for his or her own students. Differences among teaching assistants in grading standards were thus confounded with differences among them in teaching performance. Marsh and Doyle have both speculated about how these unique features of the Rodin and Rodin study could produce a spurious negative correlation between ratings and learning, and they have concluded that the methodological flaws of the study make it a poor basis for drawing conclusions about ratings and learning.

There is a more important reason for questioning the Rodin and Rodin conclusions. Their findings are an anomaly; their results are an outlier in the literature on ratings and learning. As I have already pointed out, Peter Cohen (1981) has written an authoritative and comprehensive review of the literature on ratings and learning. He found forty-one studies (including the Rodin and Rodin study) that reported on the correlation between ratings and achievement in a total of sixty-eight courses. The correlation coefficient in the Rodin and Rodin course was −.75. The average correlation coefficient between instructor rating and learning in all the courses was .43. No other study reported a correlation coefficient as low as the one found by Rodin and Rodin.

For decades, experts on ratings have been writing epitaphs for the Rodin and Rodin study, but it has refused to go away. In 1975, Doyle wrote, "To put the matter bluntly, the attention received by the Rodin and Rodin study seems disproportionate to its rigor, and their data provide little if any guidance in the validation of student ratings" (p. 59). In 1984, Marsh wrote, "In retrospect, the most interesting aspect of this study was that such a methodologically flawed study received so much attention" (p. 720). Today, twenty-five years after Rodin and Rodin published their article, we can do nothing better than to look at their findings in context. The rule is that students rate most highly teachers from whom they learn most. The Rodin and Rodin study may be the exception that proves the rule.

Do Ratings Measure Showmanship? In what has come to be known as the "Dr. Fox study," a trained actor, introduced as Dr. Fox, delivered a lecture on mathematical game theory to a group of medical educators (Naftulin, Ware, and Donnelly, 1973). Dr. Fox presented incorrect information, cited nonexistent references, and used neologisms as basic terms. Nonetheless, the great majority of Dr. Fox's audience rated his lecture favorably. The study produced a term that is still heard in discussions of ratings: "the Dr. Fox effect."

The term refers to the use of an entertaining style to "seduce" students into giving favorable evaluations to a teacher who is weak on content. The term suggests that student ratings reflect style rather than substance.

Critics of ratings have seized on this study as strong evidence for the invalidity of student ratings, but rating experts are quick to point out that the study has many methodological flaws (Abrami, Leventhal, and Perry, 1982; Frey, 1979; Marsh and Ware, 1982). Frey, for example, writes that "this study represents the kind of research that teachers make fun of during the first week of an introductory course in behavioral research methods. Almost every feature of the study is problematic" (p. 1).

The most serious charge leveled against the Dr. Fox study is irrelevance. Dr. Fox's lecture and his audience's reaction to it are a far cry from college teaching and student ratings. For example, Dr. Fox gave only one lecture before being rated. In college courses, students base their ratings on numerous lectures, the course outline, the reading material, testing, and grading. Dr. Fox might have bamboozled his audience during a single lecture, but surely everyone would have caught on to the fraud if Dr. Fox were the lecturer in a semester-long college course. In addition, Dr. Fox lectured on a topic that was completely unknown to his audience. Students in most college courses are not completely ignorant of the subject matter of the class. We can be sure that Dr. Fox would have received quite different ratings had he delivered his lecture to upper-division undergraduate or graduate students in mathematics.

My essential point is that the Dr. Fox paradigm does not apply to student ratings of college teaching. We may be able to draw conclusions about the gullibility of medical educators from the study, but surely we should not let Dr. Fox (or his creators) seduce us into drawing conclusions about student ratings. The Dr. Fox experiment is fundamentally irrelevant to student ratings of college teaching.

Do Ratings Measure Body Language? Critics of ratings sometimes cite Ambady and Rosenthal's findings (1992) as proof that student ratings are superficial. These researchers investigated what they call "thin slices of expressive behavior." These are very brief observations from which observers form impressions of others. In Ambady and Rosenthal's study, observers who saw only thirty-second silent video clips of teachers could predict the end-of-course ratings of the teachers quite accurately. The correlation between the observer and student ratings was .76. It is worth noting that Ambady and Rosenthal considered the end-of-course ratings to be a sound criterion of teaching quality, and they therefore concluded that observers can form surprisingly accurate impressions of others based on the briefest of observations.

Critics of ratings have drawn a different conclusion. If a complete stranger can guess a teacher's end-of-course ratings after viewing only a soundless thirty-second video clip of the teacher, they ask, what do end-of-course ratings actually measure? Can ratings possibly be measuring anything important? Is it not more likely that end-of-course ratings reflect only superficial expressive behavior?

It is important to note that Ambady and Rosenthal's study was a very small study that involved only thirteen teachers. The correlation of .76 between observer and student ratings must therefore have a large standard error. The true correlation between the two variables could thus fall anywhere within a range almost one-half-point wide. My own guess is that the true correlation is near the lower of these values. I base this guess on Feldman's review of the literature on agreement between student end-of-course ratings and ratings made by expert observers (1989c). The studies that Feldman reviewed involved longer observation periods and the observers not only saw what teachers were doing but also heard what teachers were saying. In Ambady and Rosenthal's words, these experts observed "thick slices of behavior." The average correlation between these thick slices of behavior and student ratings was .50. Common sense suggests that thick slices of teaching behavior will predict end-of-course ratings much better than thin slices do. I would therefore expect most researchers to find correlation coefficients between ratings and thin slices of behavior to be considerably below .50.

Do High Ratings Reflect Lenient Grading? Greenwald and Gillmore (1997) analyzed the agreement between measures of student effort, the grades that student expect in their classes, and their ratings of these classes. They concluded from their analyses that grading leniency exerts an important influence on both student ratings and student effort. They also concluded that student rating results should always be statistically adjusted to remove the unwanted influence of grading leniency.

Greenwald and Gillmore's data came from two hundred undergraduate courses at the University of Washington. The researchers found a positive correlation between student ratings of teachers and the grades given out by the teachers. Specifically, they found that teachers who get high ratings from students tend to give out higher grades, whereas teachers who get low ratings tend to give out lower grades. Greenwald and Gillmore also found a negative relationship between the grades given out in a course and the amount of work students do for the course. Specifically, they found that students reported working harder in classes where professors generally gave low grades and slacked off in classes in which professors gave high grades.

Other researchers have studied these same variables and have made several points about Greenwald and Gillmore's results. First, correlation coefficients between these variables tend to be small. Researchers typically find a correlation of about .2 between grades and ratings. Researchers also find a small correlation between student effort and ratings, but the correlation seems to be a function of the way student effort is measured. The correlation between effort and grading leniency is small and positive with some measures of student effort; it is small and negative with other measures. Second, it is difficult to interpret the correlation coefficients. For example, researchers have proposed several explanations for the correlation between grades and ratings:

- The ratings that a teacher receives might influence the teacher to be either stingy or generous with grades.
- The grades that students receive might influence them to give high or low ratings to a teacher.
- A third factor, such as good teaching, might stimulate students to perform well in a course (and thus receive high grades) and might also lead students to give the course high ratings.

Greenwald and Gillmore (1997) found that their correlation coefficients fit a model that makes grading leniency the prime influence on both ratings and student effort. The model specifies that a strict grading policy leads students to put more effort into a course, but it also leads to low ratings for the course. A generous grading policy has the opposite effects. It encourages students to slack off, but it also leads to high ratings. Greenwald and Gillmore fear that instructors, sensing the relationship between grades and ratings, may be tempted to grade higher to get higher ratings from students. One result of such lenient grading might be a decline in the amount of effort that students put into their courses. The ultimate consequence could be a "dumbing down" of college education. To prevent such a thing from happening, Greenwald and Gillmore suggest the use of a statistical correction to ratings that would remove the undesirable influence of grading leniency.

Ratings experts have questioned Greenwald and Gillmore's conclusion and their proposed statistical correction of student ratings (d'Apollonia and Abrami, 1997; Marsh and Roche, 1997; McKeachie, 1997). Among their concerns are the correlation coefficients that Greenwald and Gillmore use in their models. The correlation coefficients show the influence of the range of courses that Greenwald and Gillmore included in their analyses. It is no secret that average grades, work requirements, and ratings vary by subject in most colleges, and average grades, work requirements, and ratings also vary by course level. These factors affect the size of correlation coefficients between student efforts, grades, and ratings, and Greenwald and Gillmore should have removed their influence from their correlation coefficients. A further concern of the experts who reviewed Greenwald and Gillmore's study were the path models that they tested. The experts pointed out that Greenwald and Gillmore did not test a sufficient number of alternative models and that they gave too little attention to teaching effectiveness in their models.

Experts who have written about Greenwald and Gillmore's work find it stimulating but remain unconvinced by the conclusions they reached. The data on which Greenwald and Gillmore built their model seem weak, the model itself seems arbitrary, and the conclusions seem questionable. Nonetheless, their study will have a positive influence if it inspires researchers to explore in depth the tangled web of relationships that produce significant correlation coefficients between grades, ratings, and course workload.

Do Ratings Measure Vocal Expressiveness? Williams and Ceci (1997) studied the effects that stylistic changes can have on a teacher's effectiveness. They found that changes in vocal expressiveness produced large, across-the-board increases in one teacher's student ratings, but the changes had no effect on examination scores. The researchers argued from these findings that student ratings must therefore be invalid as measures of teaching effectiveness.

Williams and Ceci's study involved a single course and a single teacher. The course was Developmental Psychology at Cornell University, and the teacher of the course was Ceci himself. In the fall term, Ceci gave the course in its usual way, the same way he had been teaching the course for twenty years. Ceci's students gave low ratings to the course on most rating scales, and they rated the course especially low on instructor enthusiasm. Ceci's rating on enthusiasm was around 2 on a 5-point scale. The university then invited Ceci to attend a workshop on teaching skills. In the workshop, Ceci was encouraged to be more expressive when lecturing.

When Ceci presented the same course content and material the next semester, he varied his vocal pitch and used more gestures in order to be more expressive. Enthusiasm appears to be exactly what Ceci's lectures needed. After incorporating the workshop suggestions into his lectures, Ceci saw his rating on enthusiasm zoom up, and his other ratings tagged along. Examination scores, however, did not go up at all. Many people might take Ceci's testimonial to be a great success story, but Williams and Ceci present it as a cautionary tale:

> Our point is not especially that content-free stylistic changes can cause students to like a course more or less; nor is it that students' general affect toward a course influences their ratings of multiple aspects of the course and its instructor (halo effects). What is most meaningful about our results is the magnitude of the changes in students' evaluations due to a content-free stylistic change by the instructor, and the challenge this poses to widespread assumptions about the validity of student ratings (p. 22).

To Williams and Ceci, three findings point to the invalidity of ratings. First, they think that Ceci's ratings changed too dramatically in response to the small changes that he made in voice and gesture. Ceci's score on enthusiasm, for example, went up more than 2 points on a 5-point scale. Second, the rating changes were across-the-board. In addition to enthusiasm, ratings went up on scales measuring amount learned, fairness of grading, and quality of the textbook. Third, rating changes were not accompanied by changes in exam scores, which seem to the authors to be the real measure of good teaching. These are important points, and each is worthy of comment.

First, changes of the magnitude that Ceci observed in his rating are exceptional. Most teachers cannot expect to profit as much as Ceci did from instructional diagnosis and consultation. As I have already pointed out, Cohen (1980) reports that the typical teacher gains only about 0.3 point from feedback and consultation. In contrast, Ceci's rating on enthusiasm went up 2 points. Ceci's lectures apparently suffered from a very definite problem, and he was fortunate that he received exactly the consultation and training he needed to overcome the communication problem.

Second, ratings went up not only for enthusiasm but on other rating scales as well. The mean ratings for the instructor and the course went up about 1 point on a 5-point scale, and even the rating of the textbook went up by 1 point (although Ceci did not change the course text). Williams and Ceci apparently expect student ratings to be more analytical and focused. If only one factor in a course changes, only one rating scale should change. Perhaps, but rating scales reflect the way people feel as well as the way they think, and feelings are often diffuse and unanalytical. For this reason, evaluation experts usually advise teachers with low ratings to concentrate on their greatest relative weakness. Fix it, the experts advise, and the whole profile of ratings may go up. Most teachers should not expect to experience as dramatic a change in rating profile as Ceci experienced, of course, but changes in profile elevation are commonplace with highly intercorrelated rating scales.

Third, ratings but not examination scores rose in Ceci's class. This presents a problem if one assumes that ratings are valuable primarily as a surrogate for examination performance. Scriven (1983) argues that this assumption is unjustified. Learning and ratings are connected, he warns, but not in a simple way. As I have already pointed out, there is ample evidence that students generally learn more from teachers who get high ratings, but the relationship between examination performance and student ratings is not perfect. Other factors than teaching effectiveness affect student performance on examinations. Bad teachers sometimes put unreasonable pressures on students, and that unethical behavior may produce maximum exam scores. Great teachers sometimes influence students in ways that examinations can never measure.

My own impression is that Williams and Ceci have not given ratings their due. I think that ratings brought important benefits to Ceci, his students, and his university. Although Ceci's current students are not doing better on his tests than his past students did, his current students have positive attitudes toward their teacher and his course. The attitudes of his past students were negative and critical. To me, this change in student attitudes does not seem trivial.

The studies that I have reviewed here challenge the expert consensus on rating validity and utility. They suggest that student ratings do not reflect teaching effectiveness. Instead, ratings seem to reflect factors that are irrelevant or antithetical to good teaching. In the case of Rodin and Rodin's study (1972), ratings seem to indicate low teacher standards. For the authors of the Dr. Fox studies (Naftulin, Ware, and Donnelly, 1973), ratings measure showmanship. Ambady and Rosenthal's findings (1992) suggest that ratings measure little more than body language. For Greenwald and Gillmore (1997), grading leniency leads to good ratings. And for Williams and Ceci (1997), variation in vocal pitch and gestures make all the difference between good and poor ratings.

There are flaws in each of these five studies. The flaws are clearest in the studies by Rodin and Rodin and by Naftulin and his colleagues. In fact, the flaws in these two studies are so deep that most experts dismiss the findings of the studies as largely irrelevant. It is too soon to know whether the studies by Ambady and Rosenthal, Greenwald and Gillmore, and Williams and Ceci will suffer the same fate. It is true that the findings of these studies are anomalous and that experts have challenged the study findings on methodological grounds. Nonetheless, the final word has not been written on these studies. We need follow-up work on the issues they raise so that we can judge how dependable their findings are.

Conclusion

The vast majority of the colleges in this country now use student ratings to evaluate teaching, and at some colleges, rating systems have been in use for decades. It seems unlikely, therefore, that student ratings are going to disappear from college campuses anytime soon. If anything, the trend seems to be toward an increasing use of student ratings in higher education.

Given the ubiquity and longevity of rating systems in colleges, we should be grateful that a research base exists from which we can draw conclusions about the validity and utility of ratings. Guthrie and Remmers initiated the research tradition in the 1920s, and it is still alive today. Researchers continue to carry out original studies of ratings, and reviewers continue to write reviews that interpret the findings.

What do the research studies show? First, the studies show that student ratings agree well with other measures of teaching effectiveness: learning measures, student comments, expert observations, and alumni ratings. The correlation between student ratings and examination scores and between ratings and classroom observations is high. Second, research studies also show how useful ratings can be to teachers. The studies show that teachers profit from the information that ratings provide. They profit from ratings alone, and they profit even more from rating results accompanied by instructional consultation. Ratings alone raise teaching effectiveness scores a little. Ratings plus consultation raise effectiveness more.

In addition to yea-sayers, student ratings research has its nay-sayers. These are the researchers who are critical of student ratings and student ratings research. The nay-sayers have actually contributed a good deal of vitality to ratings research. In the 1970s, for example, Rodin and Rodin (1972) shook up the experts with their study on ratings and learning, and Naftulin and his colleagues (1973) further stirred up things with their Dr. Fox study. The unexpected results that emerged in the Rodin and Rodin study stimulated researchers to write authoritative reviews on the topic of ratings and learning, and the Dr. Fox study stimulated researchers to carry out a series of studies on educational seduction. More recently, researchers have presented challenging findings on the influence on ratings of body language, grading leniency, and variety in vocal pitch. I hope that researchers will respond to the challenge of these recent studies by attempting to replicate and build on their findings.

References

Abrami, P. C., Leventhal, L., and Perry, R. P. "Educational Seduction." *Review of Educational Research,* 1982, *52,* 446–464.

Ambady, N., and Rosenthal, R. "Half a Minute: Predicting Teacher Evaluations from Thin Slices of Nonverbal Behavior and Physical Attractiveness." *Journal of Personality and Social Psychology,* 1992, *64,* 431–441.

Braskamp, L. A., Ory, J. C., and Pieper, D. M. "Student Written Comments: Dimensions of Instructional Quality." *Journal of Educational Psychology,* 1981, *73,* 65–70.

Cohen, J. *Statistical Power Analysis for the Behavioral Sciences.* (rev. ed.) Orlando, Fla.: Academic Press, 1977.

Cohen, P. A. "Effectiveness of Student-Rating Feedback for Improving College Instruction: A Meta-Analysis." *Research in Higher Education,* 1980, *13,* 321–341.

Cohen, P. A. "Student Ratings of Instruction and Student Achievement: A Meta-Analysis of Multisection Validity Studies." *Review of Educational Research,* 1981, *51,* 281–309.

Cohen, P. A. "Validity of Student Ratings in Psychology Courses: A Research Synthesis." *Teaching of Psychology,* 1982, *9,* 78–82.

Costin, F., Greenough, W. T., and Menges, R. J. "Student Ratings of College Teaching: Reliability, Validity, and Usefulness." *Review of Educational Research,* 1971, *41,* 511–536.

d'Apollonia, S., and Abrami, P. C. "Navigating Student Ratings of Instruction." *American Psychologist,* 1997, *52*(11), 1198–1208.

Doyle, K. O. *Student Evaluation of Instruction.* Lexington, Mass.: Heath, 1975.

Feldman, K. A. "An Afterword for 'The Association Between Student Ratings of Specific Instructional Dimensions and Student Achievement: Refining and Extending the Synthesis of Data from Multisection Validity Studies.'" *Research in Higher Education,* 1989a, *31,* 315–318.

Feldman, K. A. "The Association Between Student Ratings of Specific Instructional Dimensions and Student Achievement: Refining and Extending the Synthesis of Data from Multisection Validity Studies." *Research in Higher Education,* 1989b, *30,* 583–645.

Feldman, K. A. "Instructional Effectiveness of College Teachers as Judged by Teachers Themselves, Current and Former Students, Colleagues, Administrators and External (Neutral) Observers." *Research in Higher Education,* 1989c, *30,* 137–194.

Frey, P. W. "The Dr. Fox Effect and Its Implications." *Instructional Evaluation,* 1979, *3,* 1–5.

Greenwald, A. G., and Gillmore, G. M. "Grading Leniency Is a Removable Contaminant of Student Ratings." *American Psychologist,* 1997, *52,* 1209–1217.

Guthrie, E. R. *The Evaluation of Teaching: A Progress Report.* Seattle: University of Washington, 1954.

Kulik, J. A., and McKeachie, W. J. "The Evaluation of Teachers in Higher Education." In F. N. Kerlinger (ed.), *Review of Research in Education*. Vol. 3. Itasca, Ill.: Peacock, 1975.

Marsh, H. W. "Students' Evaluations of University Teaching: Dimensionality, Reliability, Validity, Potential Biases, and Utility." *Journal of Educational Psychology*, 1984, *76*, 707–754.

Marsh, H. W., Fleiner, H., and Thomas, C. S. "Validity and Usefulness of Student Evaluations of Instructional Quality." *Journal of Educational Psychology*, 1975, *67*, 833–839.

Marsh, H. W., and Roche, L. A. "Making Students' Evaluations of Teaching Effectiveness Effective: The Critical Issues of Validity, Bias, and Utility." *American Psychologist*, 1997, *52*(11), 1187–1197.

Marsh, H. W., and Ware, J. E. "Effects of Expressiveness, Content Coverage, and Incentive on Multidimensional Student Rating Scales: New Interpretations of the Dr. Fox Effect." *Journal of Educational Psychology*, 1982, *74*, 126–134.

McCallum, L. W. "A Meta-Analysis of Course Evaluation Data and Its Use in the Tenure Decision." *Research in Higher Education*, 1984, *21*, 150–158.

McKeachie, W. J. "Student Ratings: The Validity of Use." *American Psychologist*, 1997, *52*, 1218–1225.

Murray, H. G. "Low-Inference Classroom Teaching Behaviors and Student Ratings of College Teaching Effectiveness." *Journal of Educational Psychology*, 1983, *71*, 856–865.

Naftulin, D. H., Ware, J. E., and Donnelly, F. A. "The Doctor Fox Lecture: A Paradigm of Educational Seduction." *Journal of Medical Education*, 1973, *48*, 630–635.

Ory, J. C., Braskamp, L. A., and Pieper, D. M. "The Congruency of Student Evaluative Information Collected by Three Methods." *Journal of Educational Psychology*, 1980, *72*, 181–185.

Overall, J. U., and Marsh, H. W. "Midterm Feedback from Students: Its Relationship to Instructional Improvement and Students' Cognitive and Affective Outcomes." *Journal of Educational Psychology*, 1979, *71*, 856–865.

Overall, J. U., and Marsh, H. W. "Students' Evaluations of Instruction: A Longitudinal Study of Their Stability." *Journal of Educational Psychology*, 1980, *72*, 321–325.

Remmers, H. H., and Brandenburg, G. C. "Experimental Data on the Purdue Rating Scale for Instruction." *Educational Administration and Supervision*, 1927, *13*, 519–527.

Rodin, M., and Rodin, B. "Student Evaluations of Teachers." *Science*, 1972, *177*, 1164–1166.

Scriven, M. "Summative Teacher Evaluation." In J. Milman (ed.), *Handbook of Teacher Evaluation*. Thousand Oaks, Calif.: Sage, 1983.

Seldin, P. "How Colleges Evaluate Professors: 1983 Versus 1993." *AAHE Bulletin*, Oct. 1993a, pp. 6–8, 12.

Seldin, P. "The Use and Abuse of Student Ratings of Professors." *Chronicle of Higher Education*, July 21, 1993b, p. A40.

Williams, W. M., and Ceci, S. J. "How'm I Doing? Problems with Student Ratings of Instructors and Courses." *Change*, 1997, *29*(5), 13–23.

JAMES A. KULIK is director and research scientist for the Office of Evaluations and Examinations at the University of Michigan, Ann Arbor.

2

The authors examine student ratings within a new framework that emphasizes six distinct aspects of validity: content, substantive, structural, generalizability, external, and consequential. They conclude that greater attention should be directed toward consequential validity, particularly how ratings are used on today's campuses and what happens as a result.

How Do Student Ratings Measure Up to a New Validity Framework?

John C. Ory, Katherine Ryan

It is fitting that as the new millennium arrives, a major revision of the *Standards for Educational and Psychological Testing* (American Psychological Association, 1985) has been completed and is the subject of much debate and dialogue. It reflects some changes in how the assessment community thinks about the concept of validity. The literature responsible for this shift began with Messick's benchmark chapter on validity in the third edition of *Educational Measurement* (1989) and continued with Shepard's article in the *Review of Educational Research* (1993) and articles on the consequences of assessment by Lane, Parke, and Stone, 1998; Linn, 1998; Reckase, 1998; Yen, 1998; Cronbach, 1989; and Moss, 1992, 1996. How validation efforts should be conducted and how assessment results are used is shifting as a consequence of this body of work.

What are the implications of this work for student ratings of instruction? We take up this fundamental question in this chapter. We begin this effort by defining the concepts that are the basis for a new unified concept of validity. We briefly summarize the past validity research on student ratings using the traditional validity framework. Based on the concepts presented, we then do a critical analysis of student ratings research using the new validation framework. Synthesizing the results of the analysis, we propose an initial agenda for future student ratings' validation efforts.

Validity as a Unified Concept

Messick (1989, 1995) has argued on several occasions that the traditional approaches to validity, which focused on content, criterion, and construct validity as three distinct subtypes, falls short as the fundamental framework for studying assessment validation. In particular, he criticizes this historical conceptualization of validity for not addressing two major issues: "the value implications of score meaning as a basis for action and the social consequences of score use" (1995, p. 741; see Messick, 1989, for a complete discussion of these issues and his argument concerning their centrality to validity). Instead, he proposes a unified concept of validity based on an expanded theory of construct validity that "integrates considerations of content, criteria, and consequences into a construct framework for the empirical testing of rational hypotheses about score meaning and theoretically relevant relationships including those of an applied and a scientific nature (1995, p. 741). Messick concludes that construct validity should incorporate any evidence that affects the meaning and interpretation of the assessment scores (1989, 1995).

What is the basis for construct validity? Construct representation is critical to construct validity. Construct representation is accomplished by using principles of cognitive psychology or theory and research in a particular subject area to model the processes, strategies, and knowledge that underlie the item or task performance on the assessment (or both).

Within this conceptualization, validity is defined as an overall judgment of the extent to which the empirical evidence and theory support the adequacy and appropriateness of the interpretations from assessments for a specific use. Critical to this definition is the notion that validity is not a property of a test or assessment. Instead validity is a characteristic of the meaning and interpretation of the assessment scores and any actions based on the assessment scores. Whether the meaning and interpretation of test scores and their use remains the same across persons, groups, and contexts is an empirical question. As a consequence, validity is not an all-or-nothing issue; rather it is a matter of degree and is an ongoing or continuous process.

Messick proposes that the fundamental principles of validity apply not just to the meaning and interpretation of test scores "but also to the inferences based on any means of observing or documenting consistent behaviors or attributes" (1995, p.741). Within this conceptualization, the concept of score is used in the broadest sense to mean some systematic summary of observed performance on assessments such as tests, questionnaires, observation procedures, or work samples. As a consequence, we believe that the principles of validity within Messick's framework can be interpreted to include student ratings, which are inferences about instructors' teaching effectiveness.

Aspects of Construct Validity

What are the central issues in validity as a unified concept? Based on a major synthesis of current and historical literature on validation, Messick (1989, 1995) presents six distinct aspects of construct validity for consideration: content, substantive, structural, generalizability, external, and consequential. In addition to clarifying some of the complexities fundamental to the validation process, he proposes that these aspects of validity be used as general validity criteria or standards for all educational and psychological assessments.

Some of the terms used to describe these distinctions in construct validity are familiar; nevertheless, we provide brief definitions of these terms within Messick's construct validation framework.

Content aspects include evidence of content relevance and representativeness. Establishing the boundaries of the domain to be assessed is critical in conceptualizing content considerations. Sources of evidence are typically results of job analysis, task analysis, logical analysis, and other forms of analysis conducted by expert judges.

Substantive aspects involve evidence supporting the theoretical and empirical analysis of the processes, strategies, and knowledge proposed to account for respondents' item or task performance on the assessment (or both). Sources of evidence include analysis of individual responses or response processes through think-aloud protocols or simply asking respondents about their responses.

Structural aspects are most similar to concerns relating to the internal structure of an assessment. Based on Loevinger's concept of structural fidelity (1957), roughly speaking, structural considerations involve assessing how well the scoring structure parallels the construct domain. Evidence involving structural considerations is based on investigations of the interitem correlations and test dimensionality.

External aspects include the familiar types of convergent and discriminant evidence from multitrait-multimethod studies. Evidence concerning the relevance of the criterion is also addressed in external considerations.

Generalizability aspects are concerned with the degree to which score meaning and use can be generalized to other populations, contexts, and tasks, including the test (assessment)-criterion relationship. Evidence is gathered from prediction studies and other studies of how particular factors (type of assessment taker, for example) might affect the assessment-criterion relationship.

Consequential aspects are concerned with score meaning and the intended and unintended consequences of assessment use. Examples in student ratings research might involve a study of how the use of student ratings scores for promotional purposes affects teachers' instructions to the students. Intended consequences (improved teaching, for example) and unintended consequences (such as watering down of the curriculum) are examined. Questionnaires, classroom observations, and case studies are the most typical methods used to study consequences.

Threats to Construct Validity

Messick (1989) presents two major sources of invalidity: construct underrepresentation and construct-irrelevant variance. Construct underrepresentation occurs when the assessment is not defined broadly enough to include critical dimensions of the construct. Conversely, an assessment can be defined too broadly and can include consistent sources of extraneous variance associated with other constructs and sources of method variance such as susceptibility to guessing. Messick defines this type of threat to validity as construct-irrelevant variance. Both of these threats to validity are fundamental issues and should be considered in all phases of the assessment process.

Needless to say, this new validation framework makes us look differently at the types of evidence required to support the construct validity of our assessments. Before we use the new framework in a critical analysis of student ratings research and practice, we will briefly examine past research efforts to establish the "validity of student ratings."

Past Efforts to Establish the Validity of Student Ratings

In the past twenty years, the collection of student ratings of instructors and courses has become the most common form of instructional evaluation in institutions of higher education in the United States. Seldin (1993) reports that nearly all colleges and universities collect and use student ratings of instruction. Student ratings are widely used by faculty to improve their teaching and courses and by administrators to make personnel and program decisions. During this period of time, hundreds of research articles have been written discussing the "validity" of student ratings. Greenwald (1997) summarizes this research by noting that "the validity of student rating measures of instructional quality was severely questioned in the 1970s. By the early 1980s, however, most [experts] viewed student ratings as valid and as worthy of widespread use" (p.1182).

Five types of research studies have been commonly conducted to determine whether student ratings of instruction can be considered valid measures of teaching quality in higher education settings (Abrami, d'Apollonia, and Cohen, 1990).[1] The five types of research are multisection, multitrait-multimethod, bias, laboratory, and dimensionality. The first type, multisection research, is used to assess the relationship between student ratings and student achievement in multiple sections of the same course taught by different instructors. Researchers correlate the section mean student ratings with the section mean student achievement scores on a common examination. Overall, multisection validity studies have shown substantial correlations with student achievement as measured by examination performance. (Abrami, d'Apollonia, and Cohen, 1990; d'Apollonia and Abrami, 1997).

In multitrait-multimethod studies, researchers assess the convergent and discriminant validity of student ratings by correlating them with selected criterion measures of effective instruction (for example, alumni ratings, peer ratings, self-ratings) across a variety of courses. These studies attempt to attribute class mean differences in ratings and criterion measures to instructors and not to extraneous characteristics such as students, the course, and setting variables. A typical multitrait-multimethod study examines assessments collected from different sources (peers, students, alumni, self) using different methods (open- and closed-ended rating items, interviews). Results have generally shown evidence for both convergent and discriminant validity (Howard, Conway, and Maxwell, 1985; Marsh, 1982b).

The third type of research, bias studies, attempts to identify extraneous influences on student ratings. In these studies, student ratings are correlated with a wide range of variables such as student, instructor, and course characteristics to determine unwanted influences on the rating process. Numerous studies have been conducted to determine relationships (or lack thereof) between ratings and a wide range of potential influences (see Braskamp and Ory, 1994, and Feldman, 1977, 1978, 1979, for reviews of the literature). The research literature reveals few, if any, potentially biasing influences on the rating process. Evidence of these influences vary in consistency and degree. For example, it is rather well accepted that ratings may vary depending on whether a course is taken as an elective or as a requirement (Costin, Greenough, and Menges, 1971; Brandenburg, Slinde, and Batista, 1977; Feldman, 1978). There is less certainty of the possible influence of grading leniency on ratings (Greenwald and Gillmore, 1997). What influences have been found "have relatively small effects" (McKeachie, 1997) and can be controlled or accounted for by the users of student ratings.

The fourth type of validity studies are laboratory designs that examine the relationship between student ratings and experimenter-controlled variables in nonnaturalistic settings—videotaped lessons, laboratory-delivered lectures, and the like. For example, different videotaped lectures may be presented to a group of student volunteers wherein they are told different stories regarding the expertise of the lecturer. By keeping all other factors constant, differences in ratings of the videotape are to be attributed to the variable (lecturer expertise) controlled by the experimenter. It is argued that large rating differences in variables manipulated by the experimenter undermine the validity of ratings. Due to the laboratory or artificial nature of these studies, their evidence has been viewed as inconclusive regarding the validity of student ratings.

The fifth type of validity attempts to identify the conceptual structure of ratings. Many studies (Kulik and McKeachie, 1975; Feldman, 1976; Marsh, 1987) have been conducted, reviewed, or meta-analyzed attempting to identify a "common" set of factors underlying the construct being measured by student ratings of instruction. Although there is some consistency across studies, results fail to identify a single set of dimensions and merely support the notion that students view instructional quality as multidimensional.

Examining the Validation of Student Ratings and the New Validation Framework

The five types of research studies have been used to collect evidence supporting the validity of student ratings. Now we will identify various sources of evidence that are discussed today in evaluating a proposed interpretation of test scores, or in this case, ratings, for particular purposes. We will then examine how well the five types of student ratings validity research have provided the necessary evidence for validity.

Collecting Evidence Based on Content Aspects. *Is there a relationship between the content of the student ratings form and the construct intended to be measured?* Analyses of the relationship between an assessment's content and the construct intended to be measured can provide important evidence of validity (Messick, 1989). To make valid inferences about scores on a test of quadratic equations, the test items must cover and represent the construct domain of knowing, understanding, and solving quadratic equations. Likewise, to make valid inferences about student ratings of instruction, the rating items must be relevant to and representative of the processes, strategies, and knowledge domain of teaching quality. But what is teaching quality?

It is this issue of an appropriate target domain where we begin our investigation of validity and student ratings. What construct domain do student rating items attempt to represent? Is there a universal set of characteristics of effective teachers and courses that should be used as a target? Unfortunately, no such set appears to exist. What Doyle (1982) noted years ago is still true today: "It seems most unlikely that any one set of characteristics will apply with equal force to teaching of all kinds of material to all kinds of students under all kinds of circumstance. . . . To try to prepare such a list entails substantial risk" (p.27).

Without a clearly defined target domain of effective instructional characteristics, how do institutions select the content for their student rating forms?[2] More important, what do these institutions infer as the meaning of their ratings? As stated earlier, most institutions of higher education report that they collect student ratings of instruction. It is fair to say that many of the forms used today have been developed from other existing forms without much thought to theory or construct domains. We have some evidence that traces the origin of several campus forms (including our own) to an item pool originally developed at the University of Michigan.

Still other forms used today are based on expert opinions of characteristics of effective instruction. Centra (1993) reminds us that Hermann Remmers and his colleagues developed one of the nation's first student rating forms by asking campus experts (typically faculty) to identify the items that were "most important to teaching and that students were capable of observing and judging" (p. 54). Similar procedures were used to develop other rating forms (Centra, 1972; Marsh, 1982a; Office of Instructional Resources, 1977).

The problem with basing item inclusion on any one of these selection methods is one of interpretation. Can we make valid inferences about instructional quality from items that have merely been grouped by student response or selected by the faculty? Or are we limited in the first case to interpret ratings as measures of "things that students use to rate instructors" and the latter case to measures of "things that faculty think are important to measure"? When we cannot say for certain what our ratings represent, we introduce two significant threats to the validity of our conclusions.

As noted earlier, Messick (1989) wrote of construct underrepresentation and construct-irrelevant variance as two significant threats to validity. As stated, construct underrepresentation occurs if an assessment is too narrow or fails to include important dimensions of the construct, and construct-irrelevant variance exists if an assessment is too broad and contains excess reliable variance that affects responses in a manner irrelevant to the interpreted construct. Both threats to validity will occur if we continue to interpret student ratings as measures of instructional quality when in fact that is not what they measure. For example, items selected by a faculty committee may place too much emphasis on lecture format or traditional methods for teaching, thereby underrepresenting the characteristics needed to teach in an active learning environment or introducing construct-irrelevant characteristics (for example, "Were the lectures clear?") to the assessment of less traditional methods.

A consequence of either of these two threats to validity is that a subgroup of individuals may be given an unfair advantage in the assessment. In our example, student rating forms that underrepresent characteristics of less traditional teaching methods or introduce irrelevant variance in their assessment may put discussion-oriented instructors at a definite disadvantage on campus. Scriven (1988) has for years criticized the inclusion of "teaching style" items on rating forms because there is no one proven way to teach.

Collecting Evidence Based on Substantive Aspects. *Does the nature of the student rating process fit the construct being measured?* When an examinee uses critical thinking to answer items on a test of critical thinking, there is evidence for the validity of the test scores. Analyzing the response processes of examinees can provide evidence of the fit between the process used to answer the questions and the process desired by the test developer. What do we know of the process used by students to respond to student rating items? Although there have been several studies (Marlin, 1987; Dwinell and Higbee, 1993; Ballantyne, 1998) of student attitudes about student ratings, we still know very little about the actual process students follow when responding to rating forms. Do students respond to items by comparing the instructor's performance to that of other instructors or to some idealized standard? What are their motivations to respond? Do they respond with a belief that their ratings will be used by the instructor for course improvement or by the administration for personnel decisions?

Research studies have indicated that student ratings are slightly higher if the instructor remains in the room during text administration (Feldman, 1979), when students sign their rating forms (Stone, Spool, and Rabinowitz, 1977; Feldman, 1979), or when students are told how the ratings will be used for personnel decisions (Centra, 1976; Feldman, 1979; Overall and Marsh, 1979). What accounts for the rating differences? What do we know about the response processes in all of these situations? If students respond more positively in these situations, are they responding more or less truthfully? Past research efforts have indicated how ratings change in different situations, but they do little to help us understand why the change occurs.

In addition to determining how students process a response to an item, we need to understand how students use the rating scales to respond. If items are presented with a 5-point Likert scale, how do students interpret and use the middle category? Do students mark a "3" to indicate an inability to respond, a middle response, or a lack of interest? If only the endpoints are labeled, how do students interpret and use the other scale points? Are some students more reluctant than others to use the extreme ends of the scale? Do some students believe that a "perfect 5" is unobtainable? To make valid inferences from student ratings, we need to determine if there is proper fit between the meaning of the scale for students and its intended meaning.

It is also important to determine if all students follow similar processes when rating their instructors and courses. Do some subgroups of students respond differently than others? Several times we have had inquiries from on and off campus about the appropriateness of using student ratings with students of particular ethnic backgrounds. For example, we have been told that students from some Asian cultures have difficulty assigning ratings because of their reluctance to criticize or to judge their teachers.

We could improve our interpretation and use of student ratings if we had a better understanding of the response process the students use. For example, if students respond by making comparisons between instructors, should we interpret the ratings of freshmen differently from those of seniors? After all, freshman are making comparisons based on only one or two semesters of college teaching. If our analysis of student processes reveals that students are more honest when they think their comments will be used to improve a course, then we should do more to inform students of the intended purpose. If our process analyses reveal inconsistent student use of rating scales, then we need to teach proper use of the scales.

Collecting Evidence Based on Structural Aspects. *To what extent do the relationships among test items and test components correspond to the construct domain?* Many student rating forms used today are based on research findings of studies analyzing student rating responses. In a manner of speaking, we have somewhat determined content and substance through empirical analysis. As mentioned earlier, many attempts have been made to identify dimensions of instruction through correlational analyses of student responses. Analyses typically categorize items into five or six factors or dimensions (Centra, 1993). Feldman (1976) established a list of twenty-two common dimensions identified on dozens of forms. Thus items are included on rating forms because they represent dimensions of instructional quality extracted from rating form data, not because they represent characteristics of effective instruction as identified in educational research. Stated differently, items are included on many forms because students appear to respond similarly to particular ones and not because they come from a known domain of targeted characteristics. It is somewhat like analyzing student responses to hundreds of math items, grouping the items into response-based clusters, and then identifying the clusters as essential skills necessary to solve math problems.

On the one hand, the number of empirical investigations examining the structure of student ratings is a significant contribution to the validation efforts concerning this construct. On the other hand, the structural studies conducted will be significantly improved when some of the issues about what construct domain student ratings actually represent are addressed. (Recall our earlier discussion of evidence concerning the content and substantive aspects of student ratings.)

Collecting Evidence Based on External Aspects. *Is there a relationship between student ratings and variables external to the rating forms that are (1) expected to be predicted by the ratings and (2) similar measures of the intended construct?* Analyses of the relationship of student ratings to variables external to the rating forms provide another source of validity evidence. External variables may include measures of some criteria that ratings are expected to predict, such as student achievement, as well as relationships to similar measures such as peer, alumni, or self-ratings of instructional quality.

Assessment-Criterion Relationships. Student achievement is the most often researched criterion variable to which student ratings are correlated as evidence of validity. The logic behind such research is that good teaching should result in high student achievement or that high faculty ratings should predict high student performance. Most of these studies have been identified as multisection studies, as described earlier. In multiple sections of the same course taught by different instructors, researchers correlate the section mean student ratings with the section mean student achievement scores on a common examination. A large positive correlation is accepted as evidence of rating validity.

The most often cited investigation of the relationship between student achievement and student ratings was done by Cohen (1981) when he used meta-analysis techniques to synthesize the results of forty-one multisection studies. There was significant variance across study results, due primarily to differences in methodology and statistical analyses. However, he determined an average correlation of .43 between student achievement and ratings of the instructors and an average correlation of .47 between student achievement and ratings of the course. Another criterion measure investigated was ratings assigned to instructors by trained observers. Murray (1983) found that high- and low-student-rated instructors were found to teach differently when observed by trained observers.

Convergent and Discriminant Evidence. Convergent evidence is provided when student ratings correlate with like measures of instructional quality, whereas discriminant evidence comes from a lack of relationship between student ratings and measures of constructs other than instructional quality. As noted, this area of student rating validity has received considerable attention. Several studies have attempted to assess the relationship between student ratings and selected criterion measures of effective instruction (alumni ratings, peer ratings, self-ratings) across courses.

Research has detected high positive correlations between student ratings and alumni ratings (Centra, 1974; Overall and Marsh, 1980) and moderate positive correlations between student ratings and self-ratings (Blackburn and Clark, 1975; Marsh, Overall, and Kessler, 1979) and peer ratings (Doyle and Crichton, 1978: Feldman, 1989). Other research results have revealed moderate positive correlations between student overall ratings of instructor competence, written comments to open-ended items, and group interviews (Ory, Braskamp, and Pieper, 1980).

Collecting Evidence Based on Generalizability Aspects. *Would the relationships, or lack thereof, found between student ratings and various external variables exist in different settings with different students at different times?* We will address two issues regarding the generalizability of criterion-variable relationships. The first issue asks whether the relationships found between student ratings and various external variables would occur in different settings with different students at different times. Would we find moderate positive correlations between student ratings and student achievement scores in all colleges and universities, with all students, in all courses? In their review of multisection courses, Abrami, d'Apollonia, and Cohen (1990) questioned the generalizability of the results because so many of the studies were conducted in lower-learning, introductory courses taught primarily to freshmen and sophomores. Commenting on this limitation, Centra (1993) concluded, "The relationship of student ratings to achievement, therefore, may not be as strong for teaching behaviors attempting to achieve higher-level outcomes" (p.63).

There is some uncertainty about the existence of the relationship between student ratings and student achievement in all contexts. There is less uncertainty about the generalizability of relationships (or lack thereof) found between student ratings and a variety of potentially biasing variables. Research on biasing influences on student ratings includes studies across many different institutions, types of students, courses, and content. As a result, most of the research findings appear generalizable across contexts and settings. The most consistent findings are summarized in literature reviews written by Centra (1993), Braskamp and Ory (1994), and Marsh (1987).

The second issue regarding the generalizability of student ratings is whether or not we can make comparable inferences about the meaning of the ratings across subjects, settings, and time. Can we make the same inference about ratings collected at different institutions or in different departments at the same institution? Can we make valid comparisons between ratings used for teaching improvement versus personnel decisions?

Some research has addressed our ability to generalize student ratings to different contexts. Studies (Costin, Greenough, and Menges, 1971; Brandenburg, Slinde, and Batista, 1977; Feldman, 1978) have consistently shown that we need to interpret differently ratings collected from students taking a course as an elective rather than as a requirement. With our Instructor and Course Evaluation System (ICES) at the University of Illinois we account for this disparity by providing separate norm group comparisons for courses that are taken as electives, mixed elective-requirements, or requirements.

At present, the elective versus required nature of a course is the only context variable that we account for in our student rating system. However, we are considering making some changes based on some old and new research revealing differences in the ratings collected in courses of different disciplines. Both Feldman (1978) and Cashin (1990) found consistently that classes in mathematics and the natural sciences were likelier to receive low ratings than those in other disciplines. Regardless of the reason for this finding, "institutions," as suggested by Cashin, "must decide how they will take academic-field differences into consideration when they interpret student ratings" (p.113). We may need separate norm groups for different disciplines. Or we may need to use a statistical procedure to control for the variance due to discipline.

In addition to differences in discipline, there are several other variables that may require some immediate attention. As we work toward providing on-line rating services, we need to consider if on-line and paper-and-pencil ratings allow for the same interpretation. Can we make the same inferences about student ratings collected in sixteen-week and eight-week courses? Are ratings of on-campus and off-campus courses comparable? We need to determine differences, understand why they occur, and learn how to account for them in our reporting of rating results to enhance the validity of our efforts.

Collecting Evidence Based on Consequential Aspects. *How does evidence of the intended and unintended consequences of testing inform validity decisions and our use of the tests?*[3] With so many colleges and universities using student ratings in personnel decisions, the consequences of their use and interpretations need to be addressed, including both negative and positive consequences and intended and plausible unintended consequences. It is certainly time to consider the consequential basis for the validity of student ratings (McKeachie, 1997).

Messick (1989) indicated that the consequential basis of validity has two component parts. The first component, the consequential basis of test interpretation, "is the appraisal of the value implications of the construct label, of the theory underlying test interpretation, and [of] the ideologies in which the theory is embedded" (p. 20). The second component, the consequential basis of test use, "is the appraisal of both potential and actual social consequences of applied testing" (p. 20). Let's examine how these components can be applied to student ratings of instruction.

The first component begins by asking about the labels given to test scores. We previously suggested this concern about labels when we questioned the naming of the targeted content domain. Student ratings of what? If we use the term *instruction,* as in "student ratings of instruction," the rating forms must accurately represent the concept—instruction. If we restrict the content of the rating items to cover only lecture-style teaching, we have misrepresented the term *instruction* and raised questions of proper inference.

The second condition of the first component requires an appraisal of the value implications of the theory underlying student ratings. Is there an underlying theory behind the content selected for inclusion on many of today's campus forms? Does the content reflect dimensions of instructional quality that are valued and supported by the campus? Sometimes the dimensions change. For example, many colleges and universities are now encouraging faculty to use computer technology in their teaching. Have the rating forms used on these campuses been modified to include technology items? The value implications of student ratings, whether intended or unintended, may be that the rating content defines dimensions of teaching that are valued and supported by the institution. How many institutions know what these dimensions are, and if they do, how many support their implicit message?

The third condition is about the ideology in which the theory is embedded. Though they may agree with the content covered on the rating forms, do all faculty believe both that students are able to evaluate instructional quality and that they should be allowed to do so? We can handle the former ideological premise more easily than the latter. We should not ask students to do something they are not qualified to do. Based on our experience with faculty and student evaluations, the one instructional dimension we do not believe students, especially undergraduates, should be asked to evaluate is course content. Most students cannot tell if a professor is teaching material that is on the cutting edge or twenty years old. However, we believe that students who attend class have the ability to evaluate all other aspects of instruction (consisting of interactions between professor and student both in and out of class, as well as assignments). We can address faculty concerns about the students' ability to judge by carefully selecting our rating content.

The second ideological premise is more difficult to address. There are many instructors who do not, and never will, believe that student ratings should be viewed as anything more than student opinion. Yet student ratings continue to be used extensively and sometimes (unfortunately) exclusively to evaluate teaching effectiveness. One way institutions can address these complexities is to develop, administer, and report ratings that adhere to sound technical, moral, and ethical standards. It is essential that rating results be reported clearly and can be easily understood. Furthermore, colleges and universities should include student ratings as only a part of an evaluation process that includes multiple measures of teaching quality (such as portfolios and peer reviews).

The second component of consequential validity appraises both intended and unintended consequences of using student ratings. Before considering the consequences, let's review the common uses made of student ratings. Student ratings are typically used in the following ways:

- To help the faculty make teaching and course improvements
- To help the administrators make personnel decisions regarding such things as salary and promotion
- To help the campus select campus teaching award winners
- To help the campus conduct program reviews
- To help the students select courses

Used correctly, student ratings can serve each of these purposes. However, their use is not without intended and unintended, positive and negative consequences. Based on our campus experiences and those of our colleagues at other institutions, we offer the following consequences, both potential and actual, of using student ratings.

Intended
- Instructors collect ratings, value the input, and make improvements in their teaching and courses.
- Instructors are rewarded for having excellent rating results (salary, promotion, awards, recognition).
- Instructors with very low ratings are encouraged by their department to seek help, possibly from colleagues or a campus faculty development office.
- Students perceive and use ratings as a means for indicating suggestions for improvement.
- Students have more information on which to base their course selections.
- Instructors use ratings as motivation to improve their teaching.
- Students perceive of ratings as a vehicle for change.

Unintended
- Instructors alter their teaching in order to receive high ratings (lower content difficulty, provide less content, give only high grades).
- The campus rewards poor teaching (lower faculty standards).
- Due to their convenience, the campus looks to student ratings as the *only* measure of teaching quality.
- The content of the student rating form may determine what is addressed in the classroom.
- Students reward poor teaching by believing they can give high ratings in return for high grades.
- Ratings are used to make discriminations between instructors that cannot be supported by the data.[4]

- Due to the high stakes involved, instructors fail to follow proper administration procedures.
- The rating process becomes a meaningless activity that is performed by students and instructors only because it is mandated.

How often or to what extent do these consequences take place? Are they potential or actual problems at your institution? Evidence of the consequences of using student ratings would come from an investigation of the existence of the listed consequences (or others that we may have missed). Through an analysis of consequences, we can improve our measures, the measurement process, and the validity of our inferences. For example, after discovering that most campus administrators rely solely on student ratings to evaluate teaching, institutions can encourage the inclusion of alternative measures, such as peer reviews or portfolios.

Future Work Needed to Enhance and Study Validity

So how do student ratings of instruction "measure up" to older and more recently identified criteria used to establish test validity? Some evidence for the validity of student ratings is provided by the results of the many multi-section studies that support a relationship between ratings and student achievement. Also providing evidence is the large body of research results that revealed few, if any, potentially biasing influences on the rating process. What influences have been found can be controlled or accounted for by the users of student ratings. It is in content, substantive, and consequential validity where little evidence has been provided or even looked for. We need to do more to understand the student ratings process and its consequences in order to support the validity of our assessments.

To improve the validity of our student ratings, we need to both improve our practices and conduct research on their use and consequences. All users of student ratings can be held responsible for acting in ways that will enhance validity. There are five major users of student ratings:

- Campus evaluation offices
- Campus committees
- Administrators
- Faculty
- Students

We offer the following suggestions for improved practice to each of the audiences.

Campus evaluation offices, or the individuals responsible for developing and supporting student ratings, must provide a sound rationale or theory behind the selection of rating form content. The items selected should represent a view of instruction (or some other appropriate construct label) that is supported by the campus as a whole. A system for the collection and reporting of student ratings should be based on sound psychometric principles and meet the demands of trustworthiness—dependability, applicability, defensibility, and relevance (Braskamp and Ory, 1994).

Evaluation offices should conduct research to determine the existence of intended and unintended consequences. The investigation can begin with, but should not be limited to, our list of consequences. Through an analysis of consequences, institutions may learn how to maximize the positive while avoiding the negative. Evaluation offices also need to continue studying the use of ratings by students, faculty, and administrators. To address the substantive aspects of validity, research is needed to assess how students view the process and respond to the forms; how faculty administer, interpret, and use ratings to improve their instruction; and how administrators are using ratings to inform decision making.

Administrators and campus committees should encourage and support student ratings by using the results in their personnel decisions. However, they must avoid using ratings as the only evidence of teaching quality or overemphasizing their value. Administrators need to be skilled in using and interpreting rating results.

To enhance the validity of our inferences from ratings, faculty need to take them seriously and follow proper directions when administering ratings. Instructors must avoid undermining the rating process by administering the forms with introductions such as "Here are those silly forms again." Instructors can also affect the way students respond to the collection of ratings by sharing with new classes ways in which they changed the course based on suggestions from past students. Students must accept the necessity of acting responsibly in rating their instructors.

Summary

This brief examination of contemporary thoughts on testing validity is intended to expand the way we typically think about and conduct research on the validity of student ratings. Recent writings on validity, especially the content, substantive, and consequential components of validity, encourage us to think more about the process and impact of the use of student ratings to evaluate instructors and courses. Or as McKeachie (1997) recently suggested, "More attention should be directed toward methods of ensuring more valid use" (p. 1218). We borrow from Robert Linn's ideas about the consequential aspects of large-scale assessment programs (1998) to suggest that the validity of student ratings is the responsibility of the various groups of users. On any campus, how students, faculty, and administrators use student ratings directly influences our ability to view them as appropriate, trustworthy, and credible measures of instructional quality. The body of literature supporting the validity of student ratings needs to be expanded to include studies of how student ratings are used on today's campuses and what happens as a result.

Notes

1. Greenwald (1997) groups the different types of validity research under four validity concerns: conceptual structure, convergent, discriminant, and consequential.
2. We use *form* to refer to student rating questionnaires. We also use *ratings* to represent what the validity literature refers to as *score*.
3. In responding to this question, we are indebted to Mark Reckase (1998) for his conceptualization of the consequential basis of validity.
4. When ratings are compared across instructors, they are best used to separate the highest-rated instructors from the lowest-rated—for example, the top 20 percent from the bottom 20 percent.

References

Abrami, P. C., d'Apollonia, S., and Cohen, P. A. "The Validity of Student Ratings of Instruction: What We Know and What We Don't." *Journal of Educational Psychology,* 1990, *82,* 219–231.

American Psychological Association, American Educational Research Association, and National Council on Measurement in Education. *Standards for Educational and Psychological Tests.* Washington, D.C.: American Psychological Association, 1985.

Ballantyne, C. "What Students Think: An Innovative Look at Student Evaluations of Teaching." Paper presented at the Annual Meeting of the American Evaluation Association, Chicago, Nov. 1998.

Blackburn, R. T., and Clark, M. J. "An Assessment of Faculty Performance: Some Correlates Between Administrators, Colleagues, Students, and Self-Ratings." *Sociology of Education,* 1975, *48,* 242–256.

Brandenburg, D. C., Slinde, J. A., and Batista, E. E. "Student Ratings of Instruction: Validity and Normative Interpretations." *Research in Higher Education,* 1977, *7,* 67–78.

Braskamp, L. A., and Ory, J. C. *Assessing Faculty Work: Enhancing Individual and Institutional Performance.* San Francisco: Jossey-Bass, 1994.

Cashin, W. E. "Students Do Rate Different Academic Fields Differently." In M. Theall and J. Franklin (eds.), *Student Ratings of Instruction: Issues for Improving Practice.* New Directions for Teaching and Learning, no. 43. San Francisco: Jossey-Bass, 1990.

Centra, J. A. *The Student Instructional Report: Its Development and Uses.* Student Instructional Report no. 1. Princeton, N.J.: Educational Testing Service, 1972.

Centra, J. A. "The Relationship Between Student and Alumni Ratings of Teachers." *Educational and Psychological Measurement,* 1974, *34,* 321–326.

Centra, J. A. "The Influence of Different Directions on Student Ratings of Instruction." *Journal of Educational Measurement,* 1976, *13,* 277–282.

Centra, J. A. *Reflective Faculty Evaluation: Enhancing Teaching and Determining Faculty Effectiveness.* San Francisco: Jossey-Bass, 1993.

Cohen, P. A. "Student Ratings of Instruction and Student Achievement: A Meta-Analysis of Multisection Validity Studies." *Review of Educational Research,* 1981, *51,* 281–309.

Costin, F., Greenough, W. T., and Menges, R. J. "Student Ratings of College Teaching: Reliability, Validity, and Usefulness." *Review of Educational Research,* 1971, *41,* 511–536.

Cronbach, L. J. "Construct Validation After Thirty Years." In R. L. Linn (ed.), *Intelligence: Measurement, Theory, and Public Policy.* Chicago: University of Illinois Press, 1989.

d'Apollonia, S., and Abrami, P. C. "Navigating Student Ratings of Instruction." *American Psychologist,* 1997, *52,* 1198–1208.

Doyle, K. O. *Evaluating Teaching.* San Francisco: New Lexington Press, 1982.

Doyle, K. O., and Crichton, L. A. "Student, Peer, and Self-Evaluations of College Instruction." *Journal of Educational Psychology,* 1978, *70,* 815–826.

Dwinell, P. L., and Higbee, J. L. "Students' Perceptions of the Value of Teaching Evaluations." *Perceptual and Motor Skills,* 1993, *76,* 95–100.

Feldman, K. A. "The Superior College Teacher from the Student's View." *Research in Higher Education,* 1976, *5,* 243–288.

Feldman, K. A. "Consistency and Variability Among College Students in Rating Their Teachers and Courses: A Review and Analysis." *Research in Higher Education,* 1977, *6,* 223–274.

Feldman, K. A. "Course Characteristics and College Students' Ratings of Their Own Teachers: What We Know and What We Don't." *Research in Higher Education,* 1978, *9,* 199–242.

Feldman, K. A. "The Significance of Circumstances for College Students' Ratings of Their Teachers and Courses: A Review and Analysis." *Research in Higher Education,* 1979, *10,* 149–172.

Feldman, K. A. "The Association Between Student Ratings of Specific Instructional Dimensions and Student Achievement: Refining and Extending the Synthesis of Data from Multisection Validity Studies." *Research in Higher Education,* 1989, *30,* 583–645.

Greenwald, A. G. "Validity Concerns and Usefulness of Student Ratings of Instruction." *American Psychologist,* 1997, *52,* 1182–1186.

Greenwald, A. G., and Gillmore, G. M. "Grading Leniency Is a Removable Contaminant of Student Ratings." *American Psychologist,* 1997, *52,* 1209–1217.

Howard, G. S., Conway, C. G., and Maxwell, S. E. "Construct Validity of Measures of College Teaching Effectiveness." *Journal of Educational Psychology,* 1985, *77,* 187–196.

Kulik, J. A., and McKeachie, W. J. "The Evaluation of Teachers in Higher Education." In F. N. Kerlinger (ed.), *Review of Research in Education.* Vol. 3. Itasca, Ill.: Peacock, 1975.

Lane, S., Parke, C. S., and Stone, C. A. "A Framework for Evaluating the Consequences of Assessment Programs." *Educational Measurement: Issues and Practice,* 1998, *17*(2), 24–28.

Linn, R. L. "Partitioning Responsibility for the Evaluation of the Consequences of Assessment Programs." *Educational Measurement: Issues and Practice,* 1998, *17*(2), 28–36.

Loevinger, J. "Objective Tests as Instruments of Psychological Theory." Monograph. *Psychological Reports,* 1957, *3,* 635–694.

Marlin, J.W.J. "Student Perception of End-of-Course Evaluations." *Journal of Higher Education,* 1987, *58*(6), 704–716.

Marsh, H. W. "SEEQ: A Reliable, Valid, and Useful Instrument for Collecting Student's Evaluation of University Teaching." *British Journal of Educational Psychology,* 1982a, *52,* 77–95.

Marsh, H. W. "Validity of Students' Evaluations of College Teaching: A Multitrait-Multimethod Analysis." *Journal of Educational Psychology,* 1982b, *74,* 264–279.

Marsh, H. W. "Students' Evaluations of University Teaching: Research Findings, Methodological Issues, and Directions for Future Research." *International Journal of Educational Research,* 1987, *11,* 253–388.

Marsh, H. W., Overall, J. U., and Kessler, S. P. "Validity of Student Evaluations of Instructional Effectiveness: A Comparison of Faculty Self-Evaluations and Evaluations by Their Students." *Journal of Educational Psychology,* 1979, *71,* 149–160.

McKeachie, W. J. "Student Ratings: The Validity of Use." *American Psychologist,* 1997, *52,* 1218–1225.

Messick, S. "Validity." In R. L. Linn (ed.), *Educational Measurement.* (3rd ed.) Old Tappan, N.J.: Macmillan, 1989.

Messick, S. "Validity of Psychological Assessment: Validation of Inferences from Persons Responses and Performances as Scientific Inquiry into Score Meaning." *American Psychologist,* 1995, *50,* 741–749.

Moss, P. A. "Shifting Conceptions of Validity in Educational Measurement: Implications for Performance Assessment." *Review of Educational Research,* 1992, *62,* 229–258.

Moss, P. A. "Enlarging the Dialogue in Educational Measurement: Voices from Interpretive Research Traditions." *Educational Researcher,* 1996, *25*(1), 20–28.

Moss, P. A. "The Consequences of Consequences in Validity Theory." *Educational Measurement: Issues and Practice,* 1998, *17*(2), 6–13.

Murray, H. G. "Low-Inference Classroom Teaching Behaviors and Student Ratings of College Teaching Effectiveness." *Journal of Educational Psychology,* 1983, *71,* 856–865.

Office of Instructional Resources. *Instructor and Course Evaluation System (ICES) Newsletter,* issues 1–4. Urbana: University of Illinois, 1977.

Ory, J. C., Braskamp, L. A., and Pieper, D. M. "The Congruency of Student Evaluative Information Collected by Three Methods." *Journal of Educational Psychology,* 1980, *72,* 181–185.

Overall, J. U., and Marsh, H. W. "Midterm Feedback from Students: Its Relationship to Instructional Improvement and Students' Cognitive and Affective Outcomes." *Journal of Educational Psychology,* 1979, *71,* 856–865.

Overall, J. U., and Marsh, H. W. "Students' Evaluations of Instruction: A Longitudinal Study of Their Stability." *Journal of Educational Psychology,* 1980, *72,* 321–325.

Reckase, M. D. "Consequential Validity from the Test Developer's Perspective." *Educational Measurement: Issues and Practice,* 1998, *17*(2), 13–16.

Scriven, M. "The State of the Art in Tertiary Teacher Evaluation." *Research and Development in Higher Education,* 1988, *10,* 2–27.

Seldin, P. "How Colleges Evaluate Professors: 1983 versus 1993." *AAHE Bulletin,* October 1993, pp. 6–8, 12.

Shepard, L. "Evaluating Test Validity." *Review of Educational Research,* 1993, *19,* 405–450.

Stone, F. F., Spool, M. D., and Rabinowitz, S. "Effects of Anonymity and Retaliatory Potential on Student Evaluations of Faculty Performance." *Research in Higher Education,* 1977, *6,* 313–325.

Yen, W. M. "Investigating the Consequential Aspects of Validity: Who Is Responsible and What Should They Do?" *Educational Measurement: Issues and Practice,* 1998, *17*(2), 5–6.

JOHN C. ORY *is director of the Office of Instructional Resources and professor of human resources education at the University of Illinois at Urbana-Champaign.*

KATHERINE RYAN *is associate professor of educational psychology at the University of Illinois at Urbana-Champaign.*

3

Through a half-century of research on student ratings, the constant quest has been to prove or disprove the existence of biasing factors. What have we learned, and what has happened as a result?

Looking for Bias in All the Wrong Places: A Search for Truth or a Witch Hunt in Student Ratings of Instruction?

Michael Theall, Jennifer Franklin

Few issues in higher education are as sensitive, divisive, and political as faculty evaluation and in particular the quality and value of the information provided by students in their evaluations of teachers and courses. Here are three statements that typify the polarity and problems in this issue. The first is from one of the most extensive and widely cited reviews of research on ratings. The second is a response by Marilley (1998) to an article by Wilson (1998) in the *Chronicle of Higher Education*. The third is a comment by someone responsible for the administration of a ratings process at a university.

> Ratings are 1) multidimensional; 2) reliable and stable; 3) primarily a function of the instructor who teaches the course rather than the course that is taught; 4) relatively valid against a variety of indicators of effective teaching; 5) relatively unaffected by a variety of variables hypothesized as potential biases; and 6) seen to be useful by faculty, . . . students, . . . [and] administrators [Marsh, 1987, p. 255].

> New evidence must be found to overturn the view that evaluations reveal who really knows how to teach, or more accurately, who knows how to make learning fun [Marilley, 1998; emphasis added].

> I provide evaluation services for my own and other institutions and I have received many requests to present the data in certain ways. One department

chair, wanting to rank faculty, asked me to produce reports of average scores to the third decimal point. No matter how good the data, assuming this level of precision is greatly overestimating the discriminating power of ratings and is grossly unfair to the faculty. The problem is not with the ratings but with their use. This is not a reason to do away with ratings. Rather it is a reason to improve understanding and overall practice [Jennifer Franklin].

As these quotes suggest, evidence exists to support the validity and reliability of ratings, but there is a strong current of opinion not only against ratings but also actively seeking contradictory evidence. One must wonder about the extent to which those who seek contradictory opinions will be willing to accept existing research, no matter how substantial and replicated it has been. Finally, the final comment points to perhaps a more important issue than the methodological and psychometric questions surrounding ratings research. It is that data can be and are misused on a regular basis. Even if ratings results were perfectly reliable and valid (and no educational, psychological, or sociological instrument provides data that are perfect), misuse would still be a major problem.

For all these reasons, student ratings of teaching are hotly debated. Unfortunately, these debates are often uninformed by the extensive research done on the topic. That research (for example, the extensive review by Herbert Marsh in 1987) tells us that student ratings are generally valid and reliable and that they can provide valuable information for students, teachers, and administrators. Even when the data are technically rigorous, one of the major problems is day-to-day practice: student ratings are often misinterpreted, misused, and not accompanied by other information that allows users to make sound decisions. When we (Franklin and Theall, 1989) surveyed several hundred faculty and administrators, we found a surprising lack of knowledge about the literature of student ratings and even about the basic statistical information necessary to interpret ratings reports accurately. That lack of knowledge correlated significantly with negative opinions about evaluation, student ratings, and the value of student feedback. We also surveyed faculty and staff in teaching centers or similar instructional support units—people with training and experience in the use of evaluation data. This group had significantly higher scores than the faculty-and-administrator group on the knowledge portion of the survey and had much more positive attitudes about students and the value of ratings information. The difference between the two groups is important taken in light of research, reviews, and applications works (for example, Cohen, 1980; McKeachie, 1987; Theall and Franklin, 1991) that have shown that when ratings information is coupled with knowledgeable assistance for formative purposes, improvement can result. Why, then, the resistance to ratings and the seemingly never-ending search for biases that might disprove their validity or value?

As the studies cited and the consensus of researchers and practitioners attests (Theall, 1994), one part of the answer lies in poor summative practice. The absence of clear policy, the use of poor instrumentation, the misuse and misinterpretation of data, and arbitrary decision making have all led to situations that contradict the literature (Theall, 1996a) and as a result, many faculty cite instances in which the established literature seems to have been disproved.

Another part of the answer lies in the psychological literature on topics such as efficacy (Bandura, 1977), attributions (Weiner, 1986), and expectancy (Jones, 1977). The notion of having someone else determine the quality of one's work is threatening, and when the evaluators of the work are not considered to be as qualified as the evaluatee, anxiety and resistance can increase. Boice (1992) documents the disenchantment of many new faculty who, despite conscientious efforts to prepare for their courses, still face student criticism. He concludes that many new faculty overprepare and concentrate so completely on the delivery of content that they exclude time for discussion, questions, dialogue, and other opportunities for interaction with students, a very important element in successful teaching and learning in and out of the classroom (Pascarella and Terenzini, 1991). Although the lower ratings accurately reflect student dissatisfaction, they can be inaccurately interpreted as meaning that the teacher is not doing an adequate job. The truth of the matter, as Boice (1992) has shown, is that some simple changes can result in increased ratings without sacrificing content or the quality of teaching and learning. However, in the face of these negative ratings and without instructional support, faculty who have prepared long and hard have to reconcile certain knowledge of effort expended against a lack of success. No wonder, then, that these faculty may develop negative attitudes toward students and student ratings. Even more serious, if the situation persists over time, a pathological pattern of behavior can develop that can lead to serious psychological problems. The stages of "professorial melancholia" (Machell, 1989) include increasing hostility toward students and administrators and, eventually, arrogance, alienation, and even possible substance abuse and verbal or grade abuse of students.

It is no wonder, then, that so much effort has been committed to seeking negative evidence. Unfortunately, most of this effort has been misdirected, trying to prove that the ratings data are biased, when it should have been directed at increasing the skills of users of the data and at correcting problems with day-to-day practice.

Reports of bias in ratings often get wide circulation (as in articles in *Change* magazine by Trout, 1997, and Williams and Ceci, 1997), but the truth is that the vast majority of these reports of invalidity or bias have been essentially refuted. Even the most widely discussed reports (for example, the "Dr. Fox" study by Naftulin, Ware, and Donnelley, 1973, and the report of negative correlations between ratings and learning by Rodin and Rodin, 1972) were unreplicable and were shown to be flawed in their conceptualization or execution. In a series of studies correcting the Dr. Fox flaws, Perry and associates (Perry, Abrami, and Leventhal, 1979; Perry, Magnusson, Parsonson, and Dickens, 1986) demonstrated that while content was always critical to learning, improving presentational skill and style resulted in better overall ratings without sacrificing the quality of learning. The studies also showed that style alone was not a substitute for content and that students recognized the difference. In the most widely cited study of the relationship between ratings and learning, Cohen (1981) found significant correlations (> .40) between ratings and student performance on common final examinations in multisection classes. Having the exams corrected by someone other than the instructors of the sections avoided grading bias. This study and replications of it form the foundation for the ratings-learning relationship, and no evidence has yet surfaced to refute Cohen's findings.

Ratings Myths and Research Evidence

There are many misconceptions about student ratings of instruction. Several writers (for example, Aleamoni, 1987) have presented these issues, but the misconceptions persist. We shall discuss some of the most common myths about ratings and look at the evidence from research on these issues. Each issue is first presented as a question, and relevant research is then discussed.

Are Students Qualified to Rate Their Instructors and the Instruction They Receive? The myth says no, but generally speaking, the answer is yes. Part of the dispute centers on the definition of the term *qualified* and on the intent of the evaluation. Opponents of ratings (Trout, 1997) essentially state that students are not qualified to rate any aspect of teaching. Individuals who are more involved in the research and practice of evaluation (Arreola, 1994; Theall and Franklin, 1990a) disagree, noting that in some areas, students are well qualified.

Students spend a full term in the course, observe the instructor in class and in interactions with students, and can accurately judge what or how much they have learned with respect to their knowledge at entry. Students can report the frequencies of teacher behaviors, the amount of work required, and the difficulty of the material. They can answer questions about the clarity of lectures, the value of readings and assignments, the clarity of the instructor's explanations, the instructor's availability and helpfulness, and many other aspects of the teaching and learning process. No one else is as qualified to report on what transpired during the term simply because no one else is present for as much of the term. Peers and administrators can visit the class, but such visits usually occur only once or twice per term, and although such visits are valuable, they cannot come close to equaling the range of events on which students base their opinions. Peers and administrators are also generally more knowledgeable of the content and thus cannot necessarily empathize with the views of students who may be having problems. Because students have this long-term exposure, it is also reasonable to ask them to summarize their opinions in some overall ratings of the instructor and the course.

But students are not necessarily qualified to report on all issues. For example, beginning students do not have sufficient depth of understanding to accurately rate the instructor's knowledge of the subject. They might estimate knowledge based on the instructor's ability to respond to questions, but this estimate is probably less valuable than a colleague's rating if the purpose is to assess the depth and breadth of the instructor's knowledge. Students are certainly qualified to express their satisfaction or dissatisfaction with the experience. They have a right to express their opinions in any case, but no one else can report the extent to which the experience was useful, productive, informative, satisfying, or worthwhile. While opinions on these matters are not direct measures of the performance of the teacher, they are legitimate indicators of student satisfaction, and there is a substantial research base linking this satisfaction to effective teaching. There is also a logical and undeniably pragmatic reason to attend to student views. They enroll in classes and pay tuition. Higher education can no longer afford to take an elitist approach that dismisses all but those who agree with its policies or procedures and who sit in silent awe at the feet of those who "profess."

Are Ratings Based Solely on "Popularity"? The myth here is that a popular teacher is not a good teacher. There is no basis for this argument and no research to substantiate it. When this myth is brought out, the term *popular* is never defined. Rather, it is left to imply that learning should somehow be unpleasant, and the "popularity" statement is usually accompanied by an anecdote suggesting that the best teachers are the ones students dislike the most. Theall (1998) reviewed comments made in reaction to a January 1998 article on student ratings that appeared in the *Chronicle of Higher Education* (Wilson, 1998) and provided many examples of such unsubstantiated claims. The assumption that popularity somehow means a lack of substance or knowledge or challenge is totally without merit. There are no studies to support this view.

Are Ratings Related to Learning? The most acceptable criterion for good teaching is student learning. There are consistently high correlations between students' ratings of the "amount learned" in the course and their overall ratings of the teacher and the course. Even more telling, in studies in multisection courses that employ a common final exam, the students who gave the highest ratings to their instructors were the ones who performed best on their exams (Cohen, 1981). Those who learned more gave their teachers higher ratings. These studies are the strongest evidence for the validity of student ratings because they connect ratings with learning.

Can Students Make Accurate Judgments While Still in Class or in School? The myth says that students can discern real quality only after years of experience in the workforce. There is no research proving this statement, but there have been several studies comparing ratings in class to ratings by the same students in the next term, the next year, immediately after graduation, and several years later (for example, Centra, 1979; Frey, 1976). There have also been studies of instructor performance over time (Marsh, 1992) showing consistent ratings of teachers by students over periods as long as thirteen years. All these studies report the same results: although students may realize later that a particular subject was more important that they thought, student opinions about teachers change very little over time. Teachers rated highly in class are rated highly later on, and those with poor ratings in class continue to get poor ratings later on. Teachers rated highly by one group tend to be rated highly by other groups.

Are Student Ratings Reliable? This is more a technical question. The myth says no; the research says yes. Whether reliability is measured within classes, across classes, over time, or in other ways, student ratings are remarkably consistent. Marsh's review (1987) provides the most comprehensive array of evidence supporting this view.

Does Gender Make a Difference? Reviews of gender studies (Centra and Gaubatz, 1998; Feldman, 1992a, 199b) have reached similar conclusions: there is no strong or regular pattern of gender-based bias in ratings. That is, students do not favor instructors on the basis of gender alone. There are a few studies that suggest other kinds of gender bias in higher education. For example, one study (Franklin and Theall, 1992) found that female instructors in one department were largely assigned entry-level, required, large-enrollment courses while males disproportionately taught upper-level and graduate seminars. Considering that certain research indicates that ratings in the first group of courses will be a bit lower, such course assignments automatically put the female instructors at risk. Further, if interpretation of ratings results simply arrayed average scores by gender, females would have lower scores. The result would be an incorrect and unfair evaluation of the female faculty. The scores would reflect the differences in teaching situations but *not* that female instructors were less competent and *not* that students were biased against female faculty.

Are Ratings Affected by Situational Variables? The research says that ratings are robust and not greatly affected by such variables (Marsh, 1987). But we must keep in mind that generalizations are not absolute. There will always be variations. For example, we know that required, large-enrollment, out-of-major courses in the physical sciences get lower average ratings than elective, upper-level, in-major courses in literally all disciplines. Does this mean that teaching quality varies? Not necessarily. What it does show is that effective teaching and learning may be harder to achieve under certain sets of conditions. The saving grace here is that the overall effect of such variables is small.

Do Students Rate Teachers on the Basis of Expected or Given Grades? This is currently the most contentious question in ratings research. There is consistent evidence of a relationship between grades and ratings: a modest correlation of about .20. The multisection validity studies (for example, Cohen, 1981) consider this relationship to be an expected phenomenon because it follows from a learning-satisfaction relationship. The multisection studies, with their correlations above .40, still provide the most solid evidence that ratings reflect learning. These findings lead to the conclusion reached by most researchers that there should be a relationship between ratings and grades because good teaching leads to learning, which leads to student achievement and satisfaction, and ratings simply reflect this sequence. Recent and rigorous studies by Greenwald and Gillmore (1997) claim that all else being controlled, giving higher grades ("grade inflation") can raise ratings. In a debate on the issues held at the annual meeting of the American Educational Research Association, Abrami and d'Apollonia (1998) and Marsh and Roche(1998) debated Greenwald and Gillmore's contentions, questioning the research and arguing that the presence of a grades-ratings relationship does not refute the established connection between ratings and learning. The question at this point becomes an ethical one: "Is giving higher grades in order to get higher ratings a problem with ratings or a problem with ethics, and should attempts to correct the problem be psychometric or policy issues?

Basic Considerations for Good Evaluation Practice

One of the first issues in evaluation is to determine its purpose. When we gather information to review or explore or improve, we describe this as "formative evaluation." When our purpose is to make decisions about merit, promotion, or tenure, for example, we call it "summative evaluation." Theall and Franklin (1990b) point out the need to consider a complex matrix of purposes, sources, and users in any summative evaluation, particularly when teaching performance is being assessed. Though it may seem obvious that summative evaluation includes more technical rigor and a wider array of data, the unfortunate reality is that summative decisions about teaching are often made on the basis of student ratings data alone. As a result, there is a great deal of suspicion, anxiety, and even hostility toward ratings.

Evaluation is a systematic process and requires acceptance, participation, and cooperation from a number of stakeholders. There are ways to develop evaluation systems that take into account the complexity and sensitivity of the process. As Arreola (1994) demonstrates, arriving at consensus about what is important, what will be evaluated, who will contribute, and what criteria will be used is the most important first step in good practice.

Student ratings are only one source of information about teaching, and teaching is only one aspect of faculty performance. Never make the mistake of judging teaching or overall performance on the basis of ratings alone. Research on student ratings has given us consistent findings, and Marsh (1987) has outlined these as definitively as anyone. But research findings generalize from a sample to a population and do not guarantee that every situation will be explained. It is critical to have an understanding of the context of the evaluation so as to be able to make fair and accurate decisions. To be fair, comparisons of faculty teaching based on ratings should use sufficient amounts of data from similar situations. It would be grossly unfair to compare the ratings of someone teaching a graduate seminar with ten students to the onetime ratings of someone teaching an entry-level required course with an enrollment of two hundred. Common sense, research, and ethical practice all demand correct interpretation and use of evaluation data.

Here is a set of guidelines for good evaluation practice.

• *Establish the purpose of the evaluation and the uses and users of ratings beforehand.* Do this by including all who will be involved in or affected by the process. Identify what is important and what should and will be evaluated, and go on to establish what kinds of data will be collected, who will provide the data, how they will be analyzed, whether all data will have equal weight, how the data will be assembled for users, and how data will be used in decision making.

• *Include all stakeholders in decisions about evaluation process and policy.* As indicated in this chapter and in the literature (for example, Arreola, 1994; Centra, 1979; Miller, 1987), developing evaluation policy or process in the absence of the individuals who will be affected is a serious error. Including sufficient time to involve the stakeholders and carrying out processes establishing consensus are part of this consideration.

• *Publicly present clear information about the evaluation criteria, process, and procedures.* As part of the a priori decision-making process and after such decisions are made, aggressively publicize the intent, purposes, and process of evaluation, emphasizing its potential to support improvement.

• *Produce reports that can be understood easily and accurately.* No matter how well designed the instrumentation, the evaluation system will face problems if the reports it generates are overly complicated, are difficult to interpret, or present data in ways conflicting with the purposes of the evaluation. Formative reports should be detailed and coupled with information and advice about the meaning and implications of the data. If improvements are needed, some suggestions for action are important. Summative reports should be clear, unambiguous, and more general and should allow users to make necessary decisions based on agreed-to arrays of data that employ accepted norms or decision criteria. Summative reports should also contain information important to understanding the context of the evaluation (for example, ratio of students enrolled in the class to those responding to the evaluation; level of the course; required versus elective status; some student demographics). Graphic displays using confidence intervals clearly showing when individuals significantly differ from comparison groups can help users avoid misinterpretation. We have identified several factors important to the design of useful reports. (see Franklin and Theall, 1990).

• *Educate the users of ratings results to avoid misuse and misinterpretation.* Particularly critical to effective evaluation is maintaining an ongoing cycle of training emphasizing the correct interpretation and appropriate use of the evaluation data. Given widespread misuse of data and misunderstanding about its interpretation, this can be the most important aspect of day-to-day practice.

- *Keep a balance between individual and institutional needs in mind.* Evaluation can and should serve both institutional and individual needs. It is possible to create complete systems for both evaluation and development, and such systems benefit faculty, students, and institutions because they ultimately support better teaching and learning.

- *Include resources for improvement and support of teaching and teachers.* This is part of a complete system and cannot be omitted. Evaluation without it is punitive. Evaluation accompanied by visible and effective development becomes a valued component of teaching and learning and the process of personnel decision making. One of the major factors in creating a campus culture and climate that support teaching is to have an established center for teaching and qualified staff to provide assistance in instructional design, development, and evaluation. Research shows us that teachers benefit most from evaluation data when the data are competently explained and when assistance and resources for improvement are available. Simply sending a computer printout to a teacher does little to help that teacher understand the results or to improve teaching. Commitment to and support for teaching from the highest levels of the institution are required if the evaluation process it to be perceived as useful and nonthreatening. Anything less results in polarized views about the purpose of evaluation and leads to anxiety, resistance, and hostility.

- *Keep formative evaluation confidential and separate from summative decision making.* Even though it is possible to develop a comprehensive system that serves formative and summative purposes, it is critical to separate the two purposes conceptually and in practice. Establish policy guidelines for the distribution and use of data, and get the commitment and active support of faculty and administrators for adherence to these policies. Allow formative evaluation to explore innovative techniques without the threat of failure. Use formative data for classroom assessment and research, but do not make personnel or program decisions without agreement about what kinds of data are appropriate and how such data should be used.

- *Adhere to rigorous psychomteric and measurement principles and practices.* Use, adapt, or develop instrumentation specific to the purposes and needs of the situation. Maintain databases, and validate instruments before using data summatively. Conduct data analysis regularly to establish norms or criteria and to clarify institutional differences across departments, disciplines, or demographic groups. Revise interpretation guidelines on the basis of clear analysis and understanding of the data. Bring in independent outside experts, if necessary, to assist in the development and validation of instruments and processes.

- *Regularly evaluate the evaluation system.* Conditions change, and the evaluation system must change to adapt to new conditions. Regular evaluation of the performance of the evaluation system is necessary to ensure that it is accurate, timely, efficient, and effective and that policies and processes are appropriate and being adhered to. When institutional or programmatic changes are made, review the evaluation system and adapt it as needed. Again, seek expert advice and assistance when necessary.

• *Establish a legally defensible process and a system for grievances.* Miller (1987) rightly establishes this as an important issue. Without guarantees of protection from mistakes or misuse, faculty and the institution are at risk. The best insurance against unpleasant surprises in this area is the work done before any data are ever collected, that is, the consensus and public exploration processes discussed in the first three items in this list.

• *Consider the appropriate combination of evaluation data with assessment and institutional research information.* Evaluation data can shed light on program and school performance and can provide important information for purposes of assessment and even accreditation. Classroom research and assessment can be supported and institutional questions can be addressed as well. The synergy of the resources devoted to evaluation, assessment, and institutional research has tremendous potential. Combining these complementary but often isolated efforts can result in better understanding of overall institutional performance, of student learning and satisfaction, of teaching and learning issues, and of other matters of importance to all members of a higher education community as well as to other constituencies such as legislators, trustees, and boards of higher education. The opportunity to take advantage of this potential should not be overlooked.

Conclusion

The principal themes of this chapter are few and straightforward. First, student ratings and other evaluation data can provide powerful and useful information. Second, good evaluation practices and the attendant benefits must be based on a systematic and careful approach involving all constituencies and achieving consensus on major issues. Third, appropriate and accurate interpretation and use of data is as important as rigorous statistical and analytical procedures. Finally, evaluation must be appropriately supported and coupled with equivalent support for improvement, recognition, and rewards. The issues, the decisions, and the future are too important to allow haphazard processes, inaccurate data, and misuse of results. Faculty, students, institutions, and higher education itself require and will benefit most from comprehensive systems of evaluation and the synergy of institutional efforts to identify and promote excellence.

References

Abrami, P. C., and d'Apollonia, S. "The Positive Relationship Between Course Grades and Course Ratings: What Is the Cause and What, If Anything, Can Be Done About It?" Debate presented at the 79th Annual Meeting of the American Educational Research Association, San Diego, Apr. 1998.

Aleamoni, L. M. "Typical Faculty Concerns About Student Evaluation of Teaching." in L. M. Aleamoni (ed.), *Techniques for Evaluating and Improving Instruction.* New Directions for Teaching and Learning, no. 31. San Francisco: Jossey Bass, 1987.

Arreola, R. A. *Developing a Comprehensive Faculty Evaluation System.* Boston: Anker, 1994.

Bandura, A. "Self-Efficacy: Toward a Unifying Theory of Behavioral Change." *Psychological Review,* 1977, *84,* 191–215.

Boice, R. *The New Faculty Member: Supporting and Fostering Professional Development.* San Francisco: Jossey Bass, 1992.

Centra, J. A. *Determining Faculty Effectiveness.* San Francisco: Jossey Bass, 1979.

Centra, J. A., and Gaubatz, N. B. "Is There Gender Bias in Student Evaluations of Teaching?" Paper presented at the 79th Annual Meeting of the American Educational Research Association, San Diego, Apr. 1998.

Cohen, P. A. "Effectiveness of Student-Rating Feedback for Improving College Instruction: A Meta-Analysis." *Research in Higher Education,* 1980, *13,* 321–341.

Cohen, P. A. "Student Ratings of Instruction and Student Achievement: A Meta-Analysis of Multisection Validity Studies." *Review of Educational Research,* 1981, *51,* 281–309.

Feldman, K. A. "College Students' Views of Male and Female College Teachers, Part 1: Evidence from the Social Laboratory and Experiments." *Research in Higher Education,* 1992a, *33,* 317–375.

Feldman, K. A. "College Students' Views of Male and Female College Teachers, Part 2: Evidence from Students' Evaluations of Their Classroom Teachers." *Research in Higher Education,* 1992b, *33,* 415–474.

Franklin, J. L., and Theall, M. "Who Reads Ratings: Knowledge, Attitudes, and Practice of Users of Student Ratings of Instruction." Paper presented at the 70th Annual Meeting of the American Educational Research Association, San Francisco, Mar. 1989.

Franklin, J. L., and Theall, M. "Communicating Ratings Results to Decision Makers: Design for Good Practice." In M. Theall and J. L. Franklin (eds.), *Student Ratings of Instruction: Issues for Improving Practice.* New Directions for Teaching and Learning, no. 43. San Francisco: Jossey Bass, 1990.

Franklin, J. L., and Theall, M. "Student Ratings of Instruction and Gender Differences Revisited." Paper presented at the 75th Annual Meeting of the American Educational Research Association, New Orleans, Apr. 1992.

Frey, P. W. "Validity of Student Instructional Ratings. Does Timing Matter?" *Journal of Higher Education,* 1976, *3,* 327–336.

Greenwald, A. G., and Gillmore, G. M. "Grading Leniency Is a Removable Contaminant of Student Ratings." *American Psychologist,* 1997, *52,* 1209–1217.

Jones, R. A. *Self-Fulfilling Prophecies: Social, Psychological, and Physiological Effects of Expectancies.* New York: Halsted Press, 1977.

Machell, D. F. "A Discourse on Professorial Melancholia." *Community Review,* 1989, *9*(1–2), 41–50.

Marilley, S. M. "Response to 'Colloquy.' " *Chronicle of Higher Education.* [http://chronicle.com/colloquy/98/evaluation/09.htm]. 1998.

Marsh, H. W. "Students' Evaluations of University Teaching: Research Findings, Methodological Issues, and Directions for Future Research." *International Journal of Educational Research,* 1987, *11,* 253–388.

Marsh, H. W. "A Longitudinal Perspective of Students Evaluations of University Teaching: Ratings of the Same Teachers over a Thirteen-Year Period." Paper presented at the 73rd Annual Meeting of the American Educational Research Association, San Francisco, Apr. 1992.

Marsh, H. W., and Roche, L. A. "Effects of Grading Leniency and Low Workloads on Students' Evaluations of Teaching." Paper presented at the 79th Annual Meeting of the American Educational Research Association, San Diego, Calif., Apr. 1998.

McKeachie, W. J. "Can Evaluating Instruction Improve Teaching?" In L. M. Aleamoni (ed.), *Techniques for Evaluating and Improving Instruction.* New Directions for Teaching and Learning, no. 31. San Francisco: Jossey-Bass, 1987.

Miller, R. I. *Evaluating Faculty for Promotion and Tenure.* San Francisco: Jossey-Bass, 1987.

Naftulin, D. H., Ware, J. E., and Donnelly, F. A. "The Doctor Fox Lecture: A Paradigm of Educational Seduction." *Journal of Medical Education,* 1973, *48,* 630–635.

Pascarella, E. T., and Terenzini, P. T. *How College Affects Students: Findings and Insights from Twenty Years of Research.* San Francisco: Jossey-Bass, 1991.

Perry, R. P., Abrami, P. C., and Leventhal, L. "Educational Seduction: The Effect of Instructor Expressiveness and Lecture Content on Student Ratings and Achievement." *Journal of Educational Psychology,* 1979, *71,* 107–116.

Perry, R. P., Magnusson, J. L., Parsonson, K. L., and Dickens, W. J. "Perceived Control in the College Classroom: Limitations in Instructor Expressiveness Due to Noncontingent Feedback and Lecture Content." *Journal of Educational Psychology,* 1986, *78,* 96–107.

Rodin, M., and Rodin, B. "Student Evaluations of Teachers." *Science,* 1972, *177,* 1164–1166.

Theall, M. "What's Wrong with Faculty Evaluation: A Debate on the State of the Practice." *Instructional Evaluation and Faculty Development,* 1994, *14*(1–2), 27–34.

Theall, M. "When Meta-Analysis Isn't Enough: A Report of a Symposium About Student Ratings, Conflicting Results, and Issues That Won't Go Away." *Instructional Evaluation and Faculty Development,* 1996a, *15*(1–2), 1–14.

Theall, M. "Who is Norm and What Does He Have to Do With Student Ratings?: A Reaction to McKeachie." *Instructional Evaluation and Faculty Development,* 1996b, *16*(1), 7–9.

Theall, M. "Colloquy, Colloquia, Colloquiarum: A Declining Form, a Questionable Forum." *Instructional Evaluation and Faculty Development,* 1998, *18*(1–2) http://www.uis.edu/ctl/sigfted.html.

Theall, M., and Franklin, J. L. "Student Ratings in the Context of Complex Evaluation Systems." In M. Theall and J. L. Franklin (eds.), *Student Ratings of Instruction: Issues for Improving Practice.* New Directions for Teaching and Learning, no. 43. San Francisco: Jossey-Bass, 1990a.

Theall, M., and Franklin, J. L. (eds.). *Student Ratings of Instruction: Issues for Improving Practice.* New Directions for Teaching and Learning, no. 43. San Francisco: Jossey-Bass, 1990b.

Theall, M., and Franklin, J. L. "Using Student Ratings for Teaching Improvement." In M. Theall and J. L. Franklin (eds.), *Effective Practices for Improving Teaching.* New Directions for Teaching and Learning, no. 48. San Francisco: Jossey Bass, 1991.

Trout, P. A. "What the Numbers Mean: Providing a Context for Numerical Student Evaluations of Courses." *Change,* 1997, *29*(5), 24–30.

Weiner, B. *An Attributional Theory of Motivation.* New York: Springer-Verlag, 1986.

Williams, W. M., and Ceci, S. J. "How'm I Doing? Problems with Student Ratings of Instructors and Courses." *Change,* 1997, *29*(5), 13–23.

Wilson, R. "New Research Casts Doubt on Value of Student Evaluations of Professors." *Chronicle of Higher Education,* Jan. 16, 1998, pp. A1, A16.

MICHAEL THEALL *is associate professor of educational administration and director of the Center for Teaching and Learning at the University of Illinois at Springfield.*

JENNIFER FRANKLIN *is director of the Center for Teaching and Learning at California State University, Dominguez Hills.*

PART TWO

Suggestions for New Methodologies

4

This chapter critically examines five issues surrounding the use of student evaluations of teaching for summative decisions: current practices, validity concerns, improving the reporting of results, improving the decision-making process, and incorporating validity estimates into the decision-making process.

Improving Judgments About Teaching Effectiveness Using Teacher Rating Forms

Philip C. Abrami

Teacher rating forms (TRFs) completed by students are often used by promotion and tenure committees to arrive at summative decisions concerning teaching effectiveness. TRFs are often the major source and sometimes the only source of information available concerning a faculty member's teaching performance.

Promotion and tenure committees have a great responsibility; their decisions often determine the course of academic careers and the quality of departments. Mistakes, either favoring a candidate or against a candidate, are costly. How, then, should evidence on teaching effectiveness be weighed so that correct decisions are made?

Anecdotal reports suggest that there is wide variability in how promotion and tenure committees use the results of TRFs. At one extreme are reports of discriminations between faculty and judgments about teaching based on decimal-point differences in ratings. Experts in the area are often shocked to learn of such decisions but do not have sufficient means to prevent such abuses. At the other extreme are reports that discriminations between faculty and judgments about teaching fail to take into account evidence of

Portions of this paper were presented as the Wilbert J. McKeachie Award Invited Address, delivered at the annual meeting of the American Educational Research Association, San Diego, California, April 1998, and the CSSHE Award Address, delivered at the annual meeting of the Canadian Society for Studies in Higher Education, Ottawa, Ontario, June, 1998. I wish to express my appreciation to my colleagues in the Special Interest Group on Faculty Evaluation and Development who provided comments on an earlier draft of the chapter.

teaching effectiveness (in other words, instructors are assumed to teach adequately), meaning that the importance of instructional quality is substantially reduced when assessing faculty performance. The correct use of TRFs lies somewhere between these two extremes.

This chapter critically examines five issues affecting how TRF scores are used for summative decisions: current practices, TRF validity issues, improving the reporting of results, improving the decision-making process, and incorporating TRF validity estimates into the decision-making process. The chapter concludes with a list of final recommendations for improving judgments about teaching effectiveness using TRFs and an example of the recommendations in use.

Current Practices

Because the use of student ratings is widespread, an exhaustive review of current procedures for reporting TRF results for summative decisions is beyond the scope of this chapter. I have, however, examined the procedures in place at a variety of institutions, including the reporting procedures for evaluation systems regarded as psychometrically sound, well developed, and widely used. I have selected for illustration a typical reporting system in place at a university with a diversity of programs at both the undergraduate and graduate levels.

The report provides descriptive data (frequency distributions, means, and standard deviations) for each item on the TRF (see Table 4.1). It also provides two sorts of comparative data: asterisks to indicate whether the instructor's results were significantly different from the norm group (STAT TEST 1) and arrows to indicate performance relative to the departmental norm group (STAT TEST 2). A sheet accompanying the results briefly explains the mechanics of the comparative results (see Table 4.2). Comments from students are typed and are also included in the report.

There are several noteworthy features of this TRF report. First, the results for both global and specific rating items are included. Second, the instructor received ratings that placed him in the upper decile of the norm group on nine of eighteen items. On three of these items, the instructor received a perfect score from the students responding. Yet on only one of the nine items was there a significant difference between this instructor's TRF scores and the comparison group.

For summative decisions about teaching, faculty members at this institution, like many at other institutions, are free to choose the ratings results for the courses they wish to include in their teaching dossier. These individual course results are included along with other evidence about teaching for committee perusal. This is the evidence the committee has on which to base its judgment of teaching quality. There is no certainty that the evaluators are cognizant of the literature on student ratings of instruction or use this knowledge wisely in forming their judgments.

Table 4.1. A Sample Teacher Rating Form

FACULTY EVALUATION

DEPARTMENT: _____ COURSE: _____ YEAR: _____ PROFESSOR: _____

FTPT: 1   TOTAL ENROLLMENT: 15   STUDENTS REPLYING: 10   PERCENTAGE ANSWERING: 66.7   #1190   DATE: _____

QST NUM	STAT TST1	RESPONSE BREAKDOWN					MEAN SCORE	STAT TST2	STANDARD DEVIATION	SUMMARY OF QUESTION TEXT
		1	2	3	4	5				
1		0.0	0.0	0.0	20.0	80.0	4.80[a]		0.42	SETS COURSE OBJECTIVES
2		0.0	0.0	0.0	30.0	70.0	4.70[a]		0.48	CLOSE AGREEMENT
3		0.0	0.0	0.0	10.0	90.0	4.90[a]	>	0.32	COMMUNICATES IDEAS CLEARLY
4		0.0	0.0	0.0	10.0	90.0	4.90[a]	>>	0.32	USES APPROPRIATE EVALUATION TECHNIQUES
5		0.0	0.0	0.0	10.0	90.0	4.90[a]	>>	0.32	GIVES ADEQUATE FEEDBACK
6		0.0	0.0	0.0	0.0	100.0	5.00[a]	>>	0.00	IS WELL PREPARED
7		0.0	0.0	0.0	10.0	90.0	4.90[a]		0.32	SPEAKS CLEARLY
8		0.0	0.0	0.0	0.0	100.0	5.00[a]	>>	0.00	IS ENTHUSIASTIC
9		0.0	0.0	0.0	20.0	80.0	4.80[a]		0.42	ANSWERS QUESTIONS

(continued)

Table 4.1. A Sample Teacher Rating Form (*continued*)

QST NUM	STAT TST1	RESPONSE BREAKDOWN					MEAN SCORE	STAT TST2	STANDARD DEVIATION	SUMMARY OF QUESTION TEXT
		1	2	3	4	5				
10		0.0	0.0	0.0	10.0	90.0	4.90[a]	>	0.32	PERMITS DIFFERING POINTS OF VIEW
11		0.0	0.0	0.0	0.0	100.0	5.00[a]	>>	0.00	IS ACCESSIBLE TO STUDENTS
12		100.0	0.0	0.0	0.0	0.0	1.00[b]	<<	0.00	CANCELLED CLASSES
13		100.0	0.0	0.0	0.0	0.0	1.00[b]	<<	0.00	ARRIVED LATE
14		100.0	0.0	0.0	0.0	0.0	1.00[b]	<<	0.00	SHORTENED CLASS TIME
15		0.0	0.0	20.0	70.0	0.0	3.78[c]		0.44	MAKES IT EASY TO GET HELP
16		0.0	0.0	10.0	80.0	10.0	3.89[c]		0.33	RETURNS/CORRECTS ASSIGNMENTS
17		0.0	0.0	20.0	50.0	30.0	4.10[d]	>	0.74	AMOUNT LEARNED IN CLASS
18	**	90.0	10.0	0.0	0.0	0.0	1.10[e]	<<	0.32	OVERALL EFFECTIVENESS

10.0% IN TABLE EQUALS 1 STUDENT RESPONSE (based on 10 students)
PROFILE FOR STAT TESTS = ALL CLASSES
FOR STAT TEST 1 * = 5%, ** = 1%, *** = 0.5%
GROUP LABEL = ALL CLASSES
FOR STAT TEST 2 << = 0–10TH, < = 10TH–30TH, > = 70TH–90TH, >> = 90TH–100TH PERCENTILE

[a] 1 = disagree; 2 = disagree slightly; 3 = undecided; 4 = agree slightly; 5 = agree.
[b] 1 = never; 2 = once or twice; 3 = 3–5 times; 4 = 6–8 times; 5 = > 8 times.
[c] 1 = never; 2 = rarely; 3 = usually; 4 = always; 5 = does not apply.
[d] 1 = much less than amount learnt; 2 = less; 3 = same; 4 = more; 5 = much more than amount learnt.
[e] 1 = top 10 percent; 2 = top 30 percent; 3 = mid 40 percent; 4 = lowest 30 percent.

Table 4.2. A Simplified Guide for Interpreting Course Evaluation Results

The > and * notations on your printout compare your individual evaluation results to the results of all the courses ever evaluated in your department using this questionnaire. The Response Profile for All Classes provides a summary description of how the students in your department are rating all the classes evaluated. Response Profiles for class level and size are available upon request.

When the Most Favorable Score Is 1 (for example, 1 = excellent, always, or strongly agree)

Arrows	Interpretation
<<	These double arrows mean your students rated this aspect of your course higher than 90 percent of the courses evaluated in your department. Bravo!
<	This means you were rated higher than 70 percent of the courses on this item. Very good!
	No arrows indicates that this item is in the middle 40 percent.
>	This means students rated this aspect of your course lower than 70 percent of courses in your department. Improvement is desirable.
>>	This indicates that on this item you received a rating lower than 90 percent of the courses evaluated in your department. Much improvement is needed.

When the Most Favorable Score Is 5 (for example, 5 = excellent, always, or strongly agree)

Arrows	Interpretation
>>	These double arrows mean your students rated this aspect of your course higher than 90 percent of the courses evaluated in your department. Bravo!
>	This means you were rated higher than 70 percent of the courses on this item. Very good!
	No arrows indicates that this item is in the middle 40 percent.
<	This means students rated this aspect of your course lower than 70 percent of courses in your department. Improvement is desirable.
<<	This indicates that on this item you received a rating lower than 90 percent of the courses evaluated in your department. Much improvement is needed.

An asterisk beside a question indicates that the response to that question was significantly different statistically from all other responses to that question. Sometimes the asterisk means that very few students answered that question.

How will the result of student ratings be used? Will committees consider all items equally important? Will teaching areas of special strength or special weakness be weighted more than students' global impressions? Is the diversity or uniformity of student responses on any item a meaningful factor? Should the absolute value of rating results be more influential than their relative value? In other words, should judgments of teaching effectiveness be norm-based or criterion-based? If norm-based, how is a significant difference important to decisions about teaching quality? How is a percentile standing to be interpreted in light of the statistical results? What weight should be afforded to the written comments of students?

One way to improve this situation is to increase the expertise of individuals involved in decision making. This has been the focus of faculty developers for years. It has not met with widespread success; stories of misuses are still heard, and some faculty still resist the use of systematic input from students in promotion and tenure decisions. One alternative is to reform the reporting system and to guide the decision-making process. Let us consider further the reasons why such a reform may be necessary.

A Selective Review of TRF Validity Issues

The use of TRFs for summative decisions about teaching depends in part on establishing adequate psychometric standards of excellence for rating instruments. Over the past several decades, a considerable body of research, commentary, and criticism has focused on issues of reliability and validity. This large body of complex literature is too voluminous to summarize here (see d'Apollonia and Abrami, 1997a, 1997b). However, several important concerns recently raised by TRF critics (including Canadian Association of University Teachers, 1998; Crumbley, 1996; Damron, 1996; Greenwald and Gillmore, 1997a, 1997b; Haskell; 1997; Williams and Ceci, 1997) are especially worthy of comment and rebuttal. These concerns are as follows:

- TRFs cannot be used to measure an instructor's impact on student learning.
- Student ratings are popularity contests that measure an instructor's expressiveness or style and not the substance or content of teaching.
- Instructors who assign high grades are rewarded by positive student evaluations.
- Global ratings, or any attempt to reduce teaching assessment to a single score, should be avoided.
- The evidence from student ratings provides weak and inconclusive evidence about teaching effectiveness that must be supplemented by additional information.

Let us examine each of these concerns further.

TRFs Cannot Be Used to Measure an Instructor's Impact on Student Learning. Recently, the Academic Freedom and Tenure Committee of the Canadian Association of University Teachers (CAUT) prepared a policy statement on the use of anonymous student questionnaires in the evaluation of teaching. The policy statement begins with a quote from a CAUT report dated May 1973: "It cannot be emphasized strongly enough that the evaluation questionnaires of the type we are discussing here measure only the attitudes of students towards the class and instructor. They do not measure the amount of learning which has taken place" (Canadian Association of University Teachers, 1998, p.1).

If I understand this statement correctly, it means that TRFs cannot be used to identify teachers who promote student learning and differentiate them from teachers who fail to promote student learning. TRFs do not tell us anything about teaching excellence with regard to important products of teaching or meaningful impacts on student growth. There is therefore no apparent relationship between the teacher ratings students assign and the achievement gains students experience as a function of the quality of instruction they receive. However, such a conclusion flies in the face of a substantial body of empirical literature designed to determine whether and to what extent student ratings predict teacher-produced impacts on student learning and other criteria of effective teaching.

Initially, Cohen (1981) quantitatively reviewed this literature, followed by Feldman (1989, 1990). More recently, my colleague Sylvia d'Apollonia and I (d'Apollonia and Abrami, 1996, 1997a, 1997b) completed a multivariate meta-analysis of forty-three multisection validity studies exploring the relationship between student ratings and teacher-produced student achievement.

There are unique advantages to multisection validity studies. First, students are either randomly assigned to multiple sections of the same course or else section inequivalence in students is statistically controlled, usually by removing differences due to student ability. Second, multisection courses with common examination procedures help ensure that course and contextual influences are minimized. The correlation between mean section TRF scores and mean section achievement (ACH) scores best reflect whether section differences in student ratings reflect instructor impacts on student learning. This correlation is also known as the validity coefficient.

We aggregated 741 validity coefficients from the forty-three studies. The mean correlation between general instructor skill and achievement was +.33. The 95 percent confidence interval ranged from .26 to .40. After correcting for attenuation, this correlation is +.47. Therefore, there is ample evidence to reject the claim that student ratings do not reflect instructor impacts on student learning. Student ratings do reflect how much students learn from instructors, to a moderately positive degree. Nevertheless, the relationship is far from perfect, and therefore TRF data must be interpreted with this in mind.

These multisection validity studies have their limitations. In particular, it is unclear to what extent teacher-produced influences on students are adequately represented by the achievement measures employed in the studies. For example, the achievement measure used may concentrate on lower-level skills such as knowledge and comprehension and not higher-level skills such as synthesis and evaluation. No studies measured long-term impacts on student cognition, and the studies generally disregard motivational and affective outcomes of instruction. Nevertheless, the studies employed the range of measures typically used by course instructors to judge student learning and assign grades.

In addition, the mean corrected validity coefficient (+.47) may not be appropriate for all circumstances. There are conditions under which the validity coefficient may vary, including timing of evaluations and instructor rank (d'Apollonia and Abrami, 1996, 1997a, 1997b). Furthermore, locally validated instruments may provide a better estimate of the degree to which TRF scores explain instructor impacts on students.

Student Ratings Are Popularity Contests That Measure Expressiveness or Style and Not the Substance or Content of Teaching. Williams and Ceci (1997) attempted to show that TRFs are substantially affected by an instructor's teaching style rather than the content of their delivery. In the report, the authors compared the TRF scores across semesters when a lecturer varied his teaching style (voice pitch, hand gestures, overall enthusiasm, and so on) in two different sections of a course while keeping course content and materials similar. Williams and Ceci concluded:

> What is most meaningful about our results is the *magnitude* of the changes in students' evaluations due to a content-free stylistic change by the instructor and the *challenge* this poses to widespread assumptions about the validity of student ratings.
>
> Our results also show that the substantial changes in student ratings we report were *not* associated with changes in the amount students learned. The substantial improvement in spring-semester ratings was not due to having a more knowledgeable instructor, better materials and teaching aids, a fairer grading policy, better organization, and so on: the increases occurred because the instructor used a more enthusiastic teaching style [p. 22].

In our response (d'Apollonia and Abrami, 1997c), we strongly criticized the research on methodological grounds, concluding that the lack of proper controls relegated the research to what is commonly known as preexperimental. We also pointed out that the research issues being explored were hardly new. They fit within a tradition begun in 1973 with the publication by Naftulin, Ware and Donnelly of the original Dr. Fox study also known as educational seduction.

Following the publication of Naftulin, Ware, and Donnelly (1973), researchers undertook a series of true experiments to explore the effects of both instructor expressiveness and lecture content on student ratings and achievement. In 1982, my colleagues and I (Abrami, Leventhal, and Perry) published a quantitative review of the research. We found that instructor expressiveness had a larger impact on student ratings than it had on student achievement. We also found that lecture content had a larger impact on student achievement than it had on student ratings.

But unlike Williams and Ceci, we did not conclude that ratings were not valid. Instead we responded as follows: "The real value of educational seduction research has gone largely unrecognized. It tells us more about *why* ratings might be valid, rather than *whether* ratings are valid. That is, Fox research serves better to probe what may produce or reduce the field relationship between ratings and teacher-produced achievement than to determine whether the relationship is large enough to be useful" (Abrami, Leventhal, and Perry, 1982, p. 458).

Instructors Who Assign High Grades Are Rewarded by Positive Student Evaluations. Greenwald and Gillmore (1997a, 1997b) have recently argued that a meaningful portion of variability in student ratings is attributable to fluctuations in instructor grading standards. In particular, they believe that instructors with lenient grading policies are rewarded with high TRF scores while instructors with stringent grading practices are punished with low TRF scores. Students may learn no more and conceivably may learn less from these high-grading instructors, yet TRF scores will make it appear as if a substantial amount of learning has occurred.

Correlational research exploring the relationship between ratings and course grades is difficult to interpret. Does the correlation between ratings and course grades reflect the validity of ratings? It does to the extent to which grades reflect differences in what students have learned as a function of instruction. It does not to the extent to which grades reflect differences in how instructors assign grades. Research, then, needs to differentiate effects attributable to differences in instructor grading standards from effects attributable to instructor impacts on student learning. In addition, other potential sources of influence need to be accounted for, including differences in grades and ratings attributable to student factors. (For a thorough critique and reinterpretation of Greenwald and Gillmore, see Marsh and Roche, 1998).

While attempts to unequivocally disentangle these different influences in correlational research have been unsuccessful, the same cannot be said of several field and laboratory experiments that offer greater control over instructor and grading characteristics. One such experiment (Abrami, Dickens, Perry, and Leventhal, 1980) explored the effects of differences in instructor grading standards on student rating and achievement for instructors who varied in both expressiveness and lecture content. We found weak and inconsistent effects of grading standards. Quite surprisingly, we even found one condition where assigning higher grades resulted in the instructor's being assigned significantly lower student evaluations.

More recently, colleagues and I (d'Apollonia, Lou, and Abrami; 1998) conducted a meta-analysis on field and laboratory experiments designed to examine the influence of instructor grading standards on student ratings. We computed 140 effect sizes from nine studies. The average effect size was +.22, a small effect (that is, less than one-quarter standard deviation) suggesting that instructor grading standards do slightly affect student ratings. But in addition to the average effect being small, we also found the effects to be significantly variable. In other words, the effect is not always the same size or even in the same direction. We concluded that there is no evidence of meaningful, widespread variability in instructor grading standards. Furthermore, we suggested that statistical adjustments are not warranted because the grading standards effect appears to be small on average, variable, and not readily separable from the valid influences of instructors on ratings.

Global Ratings, or Any Attempt to Reduce Teaching Assessment to a Single Score, Should Be Avoided. Teaching is multifaceted—so multifaceted, I believe, that any attempt to try to capture the breadth and complexity of teaching in a single, multidimensional rating form is doomed.

In contrast, summative decisions about teaching effectiveness are not multifaceted. Although committees may need to consider multiple sources of information, their decisions about effective teaching are often described along a single dimension of teaching excellence ranging from poor to outstanding.

My colleagues and I (Abrami, d'Apollonia, and Rosenfield, 1996) attempted to determine two things: whether and how many teaching dimensions were common among a collection of student ratings and the factor structure of the dimensions that were common to the forms.

We began by categorizing 485 items from seventeen rating forms into one of forty categories. We next examined the homogeneity of over twenty thousand interitem correlations subdivided into these categories. Pruning to reduce heterogeneity led to the elimination of a large number of items and several categories. We were left with thirty-five categories, 225 items, and fewer than seven thousand correlations.

We next factor-analyzed the aggregate correlation matrix. It resulted in a four-factor solution of which the first factor accounted for more than 60 percent of the variance on which almost all of the categories loaded. Together the three remaining factors accounted for about 10 percent of the variance. We concluded that there is a large general factor common to student ratings and therefore a general factor of global items should be used for summative decisions about teaching.

Student Ratings Provide Weak and Inconclusive Evidence About Teaching Effectiveness That Must Be Supplemented by Additional Information. Is the evidence on student ratings weak and inconclusive, as critics contend, or strong and conclusive, as proponents suggest? Global student ratings are moderately good, but not perfect, predictors of teacher impacts on student learning. They may be very slightly and inconsistently affected by several factors, including instructor expressiveness and grading standards. To be used properly, TRFs should be used to make general judgments about teaching effectiveness.

Other evidence of teaching effectiveness should also be used in making summative decisions. Additional sources of evidence include alumni ratings, peer ratings, self-ratings, chair ratings, course outlines, evidence of student productivity, and teaching portfolios. These additional sources should be subject to the same scrutiny as student ratings. Are they reliable and valid? Are the data representative?

But other sources often are less psychometrically sound than TRFs. For example, selective evidence of student productivity provided by the instructor is a questionable source of evidence of teaching effectiveness. Are the samples representative of the class as a whole? How can the effects of instructor ability be separated from the effects of student ability when these data are used for summative decisions about teaching effectiveness?

Improving the Reporting of Results

The reporting system should present the best evidence for summative decisions as clearly as possible. In this section, I will discuss what should be included in reporting the results of TRFs. In a later section, I will suggest ways of best presenting these results visually.

Based on our research (see Abrami, d'Apollonia, and Rosenfield, 1996; d'Apollonia and Abrami, 1997a, 1997b), the reporting system for summative decisions should not include the results of individual, specific TRF items. The results of individual-specific items are best used for teaching improvement purposes, that is, for formative decisions about teaching. The reporting system for summative decisions should include the results of individual global items or, preferably, the reporting of an average of several global items. In the absence of global items, the weighted average of specific items may be substituted.

Furthermore, as will be explained shortly, it is preferable to combine the results for a faculty member's courses than to present them separately. Combining the results improves the power of subsequent statistical tests. It should be decided in advance whether the combined course ratings are weighted by the number of students per course or unweighted. Weighting allows each student per course an equal voice in the combined ratings. Not weighting allows each course to be given the same importance in the combined ratings regardless of class size.

Freedom to select the courses to be included in a teaching dossier for summative decisions about teaching is empowering for individual faculty, but it does not ensure that good decisions about teaching will be made. It tends to discredit the evaluation process and may even be unfair to faculty who are less bold about discarding low ratings. Therefore, I recommend one of the following alternatives be chosen and made to apply to all faculty:

1. Include course evaluations for all courses.
2. Include all courses after they have been taught at least once.
3. Include all courses except two.
4. Include the same prescribed number of courses for all faculty.

Including all of the data or being consistent about which data are selected ensures that rating results are a representative and fair sample of student opinions about teaching effectiveness. This desire for uniformity also underlies the common practice of recommending similar conditions for data collection (time of year, student anonymity, and so on)

With regard to selectivity, I am reminded of the clinician who expressed dismay when the results of statistical testing revealed that patients receiving her experimental treatment fared no better than control patients. "These results are meaningless. Of course the treatment works. Just look at how much improvement some of the experimental patients showed."

Note that twenty years ago, I would have argued against my own recommendations. Why set up a set of procedures designed to eliminate so much of the faculty member's and committee's autonomy in presenting and interpreting the data? Why obscure so much of individual course and setting influences? In my opinion, current complaints about the misuse of student ratings in summative evaluations are a result of flexible and detailed reporting systems. Time, unfortunately, has proved my initial position wrong.

Improving the Decision-Making Process

We need to be concerned not only with the data reported but also with how these data are used to make promotion and merit decisions. It is amusing that when social scientists are provided with research evidence, they do not hesitate to apply statistical hypothesis-testing procedures to the data. Yet when the situation involves not research but a decision about teaching effectiveness, seldom do these same social scientists give a thought to applying these statistical procedures. And if the social scientists do not proceed in a statistically rigorous fashion, it should hardly be surprising that faculty from other disciplines also fail to do so. I shall summarize ways to apply statistical hypothesis-testing procedures to summative decisions about teaching effectiveness.

Hypothesis Testing: Restating the Obvious? The problem of making correct decisions about faculty teaching effectiveness can be viewed from the perspective of statistical hypothesis testing. In my opinion, proper use of statistical hypothesis-testing procedures will lead to better summative decisions about teaching. In statistical hypothesis testing, one follows these steps:

1. State the null hypothesis.
2. State the alternative hypothesis.
3. Select a probability value for significance testing.
4. Select the appropriate test statistic.
5. Compute the calculated value.
6. Determine the critical value.
7. Compare the calculated value and the critical value to choose between the null hypothesis and the alternative hypothesis.

I will elaborate on these steps from two perspectives: norm-referenced and criterion-referenced evaluation.

Norm-Referenced Versus Criterion-Referenced Evaluation. Two types of questions about teaching effectiveness can be made into hypotheses: norm-referenced and criterion-referenced. A norm-referenced question about teaching effectiveness is concerned with how individual faculty compare to an appropriate collection of faculty. A criterion-referenced question about teaching effectiveness is concerned with how individual faculty compare to a predetermined standard of excellence.

Researchers and faculty developers have debated the merits of norm-referenced versus criterion-referenced standards for assessing teaching effectiveness (Abrami, 1993; Aleamoni, 1996; Cashin, 1992, 1994, 1996; Hativa, 1993; McKeachie, 1996; Theall, 1996). Among the reasons for using norm groups is that they allow decisions makers to judge individual teaching quality in comparison to what other faculty have been able to accomplish in comparable contexts (similar courses, students, disciplines, and so on). Among the reasons against using norm groups are that establishing appropriate norm groups can be difficult, leading to biased comparisons, and the nature of normative comparisons engenders competition among faculty. Among the reasons for using criterion referencing is that it provides clear and absolute standards for teaching quality that do not depend on the performance of others but can still be adjusted to reflect the teaching context. Among the reasons against using criterion referencing are that it is difficult to establish criteria of teaching effectiveness in the absence of normative data and that TRF data are skewed, raising the possibility of a positive bias in student ratings (students judge teachers more kindly then they should).

Given the advantages and disadvantages of both norm and criterion referencing, statistical procedures will be given for both. We will discuss norm-based questions first.

Hypothesis-Testing Procedures for Norm-Referenced Evaluation. Here is an example of a norm-based null hypothesis and an alternative to it:

$$H_0: \mu_i = \mu_g$$
$$H_a: \mu_i \neq \mu_g$$

where H_0 is the null hypothesis and H_a is the alternative hypothesis, μ_i is the mean TRF score for an individual faculty member, and μ_g is the mean TRF score for the comparison group of faculty.

There are likely to be situations where the alternative hypothesis is a directional or one-tailed alternative (for example, $H_a: \mu_i < \mu_g$ for a tenure decision or $H_a: \mu_i > \mu_g$ for a merit award).

The probability value for significance testing should be set in advance, prior to viewing or analyzing the data. Social scientists seldom use probability values larger than .05. It remains for the review committee (and possibility the university administration and faculty union) to decide this matter.

I know of few instances where these decisions were made in advance by a review committee. This failure may explain why some summative decisions are based on fine (that is, nonsignficant) differences between faculty ratings and a norm-based or criterion-based standard. Next, assuming that the TRF data meet acceptable standards, parametric statistical tests such as the t-test may be employed.

Norm-Based Statistical Procedures. Here is an example of a norm-based t-test:

$$t = \frac{\bar{Y}_i - \bar{Y}_g}{\sqrt{\frac{s_i^2}{n_i} + \frac{s_g^2}{n_g}}} \text{ for } df = n_i + n_g - 2$$

where $\bar{Y}$ is the mean TRF score, s^2 is the unbiased variance, n is the sample size, and df is the degrees of freedom.

In addition, one can calculate a confidence interval for the calculated value of t:

$$CI = (\bar{Y}_i - \bar{Y}_g) \pm t_\alpha s_D$$

where t_α is the critical value of t at a particular alpha level. Also:

$$s_D = \sqrt{\frac{s_i^2}{n_i} + \frac{s_g^2}{n_g}} .$$

Why TRF Scores Should Be Combined. Since summative decisions are often based on a collection of faculty TRFs, the mean, variance, and sample size for an individual faculty member should be combined from several courses and a single t-test calculated. To avoid confusion in decision making arising from multiple test results and to increase statistical power, it is inadvisable to conduct statistical tests for each course separately. Individual course results may be more useful for formative purposes, whereas combined course results are more useful for summative purposes. In summative evaluation, we want to make a decision about the instructor's general teaching ability from prior evidence in order to make an inference about the expected quality of the instructor's teaching in the future. Unfortunately, multiple significance tests of individual courses are the more common practice than combining all the data for a faculty member and conducting a single significance test.

Consider the following scenario. A new faculty member teaches several courses during his or her first years in the department. Each course is evaluated, and the professor's TRF scores are compared to universitywide ratings. The tenure committee decides to determine whether the faculty member's course evaluations are significantly ($p < .05$) worse than average (H_a: $\mu_i < \mu_g$).

For the sake of simplicity, let us assume that the class size for the faculty member is always twenty students, that the mean TRF rating in each class is always 4.00 with a standard deviation of 0.50, and that there are data for ten classes. Furthermore, let us assume that the normative data resemble those for the IDEA evaluation system (Cashin, 1998): mean TRF = 4.17, $s = .67$, $n = 40,000$.

First consider the ten courses separately:

$$t = \frac{4.00 - 4.17}{\sqrt{\dfrac{.50^2}{20} + \dfrac{.67^2}{40,000}}} = \frac{-0.17}{.11} = -1.55.$$

CI = -0.17 ± 1.65 (.04) = $-0.24, -0.10$ expressed as mean differences or
3.93, 4.07 expressed as raw scores,

which does not exceed the critical value -1.65.

$$CI = (\bar{Y}_i - \bar{Y}_g) \pm t_\alpha s_D$$

CI = -0.17 ± 1.65 (.11) = $-0.35, +0.01$ expressed as mean differences or
3.82, 4.18 expressed as raw scores.

In this example, this result and conclusion would be repeated ten times.

Now consider the ten courses together:

$$t = \frac{4.00 - 4.17}{\sqrt{\dfrac{.50^2}{200} + \dfrac{.67^2}{40,000}}} = \frac{-0.17}{.04} = -4.25,$$

which does exceed the critical value of -1.65.

What accounts for the difference between the examples? Differences in sample size are the key. The small sample size for each course versus the large sample size for the courses combined explains the different statistical outcomes.

Failure to combine TRF data for a professor increases the risk of Type II errors. All other things being equal, the increased sample sizes for pooled data decrease the tendency of failing to reject the null hypothesis when it should be rejected.

Visual Displays of Normative Data. The visual display of data can aid in the interpretation of TRF results, especially for individuals lacking knowledge of statistics. A useful visual display should include the distribution of normative data, noting the norm group mean along with percentile, z-score, and raw score equivalents, which serve as informative points on the distribution. In addition to these normative data, the combined mean score for the faculty member and the confidence interval should be overlaid.

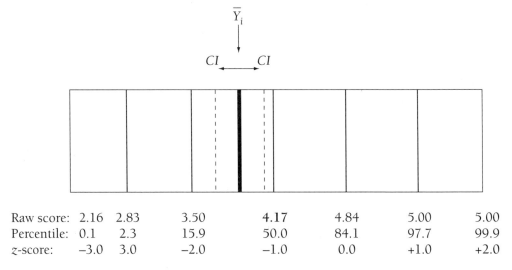

Raw score:	2.16	2.83	3.50	4.17	4.84	5.00	5.00
Percentile:	0.1	2.3	15.9	50.0	84.1	97.7	99.9
z-score:	−3.0	3.0	−2.0	−1.0	0.0	+1.0	+2.0

The dark solid line shows the combined mean TRF score for a faculty member. The dashed lines represents the 95 percent confidence interval surrounding the significance test of mean differences. The visual display shows that the faculty member has significantly lower TRF scores than the norm group. The upper limit of the 95 percent confidence interval (4.07 expressed as a raw score) falls below the average score, which is boldfaced, for all faculty combined (4.17 expressed as a raw score). Note that because skewed and otherwise nonnormal distributions are possible, the raw score and percentile equivalents should be determined from the actual distribution of data rather than from the theoretical distribution I used here.

What about other comparisons? Normative data may be used to explore statistically hypotheses other than whether the mean TRF score for one professor differs significantly from the mean score of the collection of professors. In a symmetrical distribution, the norm group mean represents the 50th percentile. But what if the decision is made, a priori, to evaluate the hypothesis that a faculty member's mean TRF is significantly lower than a particular percentile rank other than the 50th?

H_0: μ_i = 25%ile
H_a: μ_i < 25%ile

Imagine that a negative decision will be made about teaching effectiveness if the faculty member's mean ratings fall significantly below 75 percent of the ratings of the norm group, that is, in the lowest 25th percentile. In the current example, the theoretical distribution of scores suggests that the value associated with the 25th percentile is 3.71. Therefore, if we use the data from the previous example but modify the norm group mean to reflect the 25th percentile, we obtain the following:

$$t = \frac{\bar{Y}_i - 25\%ile}{\sqrt{\dfrac{s_i^2}{n_i} + \dfrac{s_g^2}{n_g}}} = \frac{4.00 - 3.71}{\sqrt{\dfrac{.50^2}{200} + \dfrac{.67^2}{40,000}}} = \frac{0.29}{.04} = 7.25$$

$$CI = (\bar{Y}_i - 25\%ile) \pm t_\alpha s_D$$

CI = +0.29 $\pm$ 1.65 (.04) = +0.22, +0.36 expressed as mean differences or 3.93, 4.07 expressed as raw scores.

In this example, the null hypothesis is not rejected in favor of the directional alternative hypothesis because the mean difference is in the "wrong" direction. The instructor's mean rating is actually higher than the 25th percentile, and one cannot conclude that this instructor's teaching was inferior.

Another hypothesis that can be explored is whether two professors' teaching performance is significantly different. Such a comparison is likely when candidates are being considered for a teaching award.

Hypothesis-Testing Procedures for Criterion-Referenced Evaluation. An example of criterion-based null and alternative hypotheses is as follows:

H_0: $\mu_i = \chi$
H_a: $\mu_i \neq \chi$

where H_0 is the null hypothesis and H_a is the alternative hypothesis, μ_i is the mean TRF score for an individual faculty member, and χ is the criterion TRF score.

There are likely to be situations where the alternative hypothesis is a directional or one-tailed alternative (for example, H_a: $\mu_i < \chi$ for a tenure decision or H_a: $\mu_i > \chi$ for a merit award).

The probability value for significance testing should be set in advance, prior to viewing or analyzing the data. Social scientists seldom use probability values larger than .05. It remains for the review committee (and possibly the university administration and faculty union) to decide this matter and to set the teaching performance criterion.

Criterion-Based Statistical Procedures. Here is an example of a criterion-based t-test:

$$t = \frac{\bar{Y}_i - C}{\sqrt{s_i^2/n_i}} \quad \text{for} \quad df = n_i - 1$$

where $\bar{Y}$ is the mean TRF score, C is the criterion score, s^2 is the unbiased variance, n is sample size, and df is the degrees of freedom.

In addition, one can calculate a confidence interval for the calculated value of t:

$$CI = (\bar{Y}_i - \bar{Y}_g) \pm t_\alpha s_C$$

where t_α is the critical value of t at a particular alpha level and

$$s_C = \sqrt{s_i^2/n_i}$$

Why TRF Scores Should Be Combined. The low power of statistical tests based on individual courses also exists in the case of criterion-referenced evaluation. Let us consider the previous scenario but assume that criterion-based evaluation will occur. The tenure committee decides to determine whether the faculty member's course evaluations are significantly ($p < .05$) worse than 4.15 (H_a: $\mu_i < 4.15$).

First consider the ten courses separately:

$$t = \frac{4.00 - 4.15}{\sqrt{.50^2/20}} = \frac{-0.15}{.11} = -1.36,$$

$$CI = (\bar{Y}_i - \bar{Y}_g) \pm t_\alpha s_D$$

which does not exceed the critical value −1.65.

CI = −0.15 ± 1.65 (.11) = −0.33, +0.03 expressed as mean differences or 3.82, 4.18 expressed as raw scores.

In this example, this result and conclusion would be repeated ten times. In each case, we fail to reject the null hypothesis that there is no difference between the instructor's teaching performance and the criterion.

Now consider the ten courses together:

$$t = \frac{4.00 - 4.15}{\sqrt{.50^2/200}} = \frac{-0.15}{.04} = -3.75,$$

which does exceed the critical value −1.65.

CI = −0.15 ± 1.65 (.04) = −0.22, −0.08 expressed as mean differences or 3.93, 4.08 expressed as raw scores.

In other words, one can be 95 percent certain that the difference between the professor's combined data mean and the criterion score is as large as −0.22 and as small as −0.08. We reject the null hypothesis and conclude that the instructor's teaching performance is substandard.

With criterion referencing, the failure to combine TRF data for a professor increases the risk of Type II errors. All other things being equal, the increased sample sizes for pooled data decrease the tendency of failing to reject the null hypothesis when it should be rejected.

Visual Displays of Criterion Data. The visual display of data can aid in the interpretation of TRF results when criterion referencing is used. A useful visual display should include the scale points used on the rating form with the criterion noted. In addition, the combined mean score for the faculty member and the confidence interval should be overlaid.

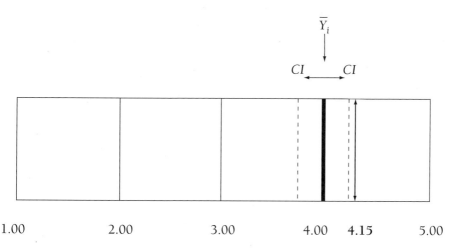

| 1.00 | 2.00 | 3.00 | 4.00 | 4.15 | 5.00 |

The dark solid line shows the combined mean TRF score for a faculty member. The dashed lines represents the confidence interval surrounding the significance test. The solid line with arrows in the rectangle represents the teaching performance criterion.

The visual display shows that the faculty member has a significantly lower mean TRF score than the criterion, which is boldfaced; it also shows the 95 percent confidence interval in which the mean score lies.

Incorporating TRF Validity Estimates into the Decision Process

Why are fine distinctions among TRF results to be avoided? Decades of research on TRFs suggest that while they reflect student opinion with reasonable accuracy, ratings only moderately explain the extent to which teachers promote student learning. As mentioned, in a recent meta-analysis of multisection validity studies, my colleague and I (d'Apollonia and Abrami, 1997b) reported a mean correlation of +.33 between student ratings of general instructor skill and teacher-produced student learning. After correcting for attenuation, the mean correlation was +.47.

I would therefore like to suggest a way to use evidence concerning the validity of student ratings, particularly the validity coefficient, to help educators make wiser decisions about teaching quality. This recommendation follows from the belief that administrative uses of TRF results require improvement. Decision makers have failed, in part, to take advantage of the available evidence on the reliability and validity evidence and to use student ratings wisely. In light of this failure, I propose some alternatives.

Classic Measurement Theory. The essence of my suggestion is derived from classic measurement theory. In classic measurement theory, a *true score* is a hypothetical value that best represents an individual's true skill, ability, or attribute. It is a value that can be depended on to yield consistent knowledge of individual differences unaffected by the inexactitudes of measurement such as practice effects, response set, and other influences that contribute to imprecise and unstable test scores. For faculty, a true score is a hypothetical value that best represents an individual's true teaching effectiveness.

In practice, of course, a true score can never be known, but it can be estimated. The best estimate of a person's true score is the *obtained score*. Unfortunately, obtained scores sometimes underestimate or overestimate corresponding true scores.

The difference between an obtained score and an individual's true score is the *error score*. The error score represents chance or unexplained fluctuation in test scores. These unexplained influences may sometimes operate to either increase or decrease obtained scores. Therefore, an obtained score may be thought of as having two components:

Obtained score = true score + error score.

For faculty, an obtained TRF score represents some portion that is their true teaching effectiveness and some portion that is error or chance fluctuation:

TRF score = teaching effectiveness + error.

Reliability. Technically, a test's *reliability coefficient* is used to estimate the relationship between true scores and obtained scores. More precisely, the square root of the reliability coefficient estimates the correlation between obtained and true scores. For example, if the test-retest reliability coefficient is .81, the estimated correlation between obtained and true scores is .90.

TRFs have good internal consistency and stability. That is, the items on TRFs are homogeneous and correlate well with one another (they have internal consistency). TRFs scores are also highly correlated from one administration to another (they have stability). Reliability coefficients are usually .80 or higher (Feldman, 1977).

Another type of reliability is test equivalence or alternate forms. In the traditional sense, alternate forms reliability is the correlation between two versions of the same instrument. Alternate forms reliability for TRFs might include the correlation between mean TRF scores from different instruments or the correlation between mean TRF factor scores from different instruments purporting to measure the same teaching behaviors (for example, skill, enthusiasm, or rapport).

I would urge that we consider another possibility. Instead of using teacher-produced student learning as a criterion, what would happen if we considered it as an alternative form of measuring teaching effectiveness? Then the TRF-ACH correlation could be used to determine the extent to which the obtained mean TRF scores are influenced by error. That is, we would consider the extent to which mean TRF scores and mean ACH scores are not perfectly related as an indication of error in the obtained mean TRF scores and a departure from hypothetical true scores.

This way of thinking about the TRF-ACH correlation is a departure from traditional notions, which view this correlation as indicative of criterion validity. It takes some license with traditional notions from measurement theory. But it provides us with a great advantage. Let us see, then, what can be made of the TRF-ACH correlation as a measure of equivalence.

Standard Error of Measurement. The standard deviation of error scores is the extent to which a set of test scores fluctuates as a function of chance. When obtained scores match true scores and error is low, there is little fluctuation, which is a function of error. The standard deviation of the error scores is also known as the standard error of measurement (s_m).

The s_m can be estimated from knowledge of the variability in the obtained scores and the reliability of the test. More precisely:

$$s_m = s\sqrt{(1 - rel)}$$

where s is the standard deviation of the set of scores and rel is the test reliability.

When test reliability is high, s_m is small. When test reliability is low, s_m is high. Only when there is no error of measurement is there no need to estimate the extent to which obtained, individual test scores fluctuate as a function of chance (and therefore obtained scores equal true scores).

Using the Measure of Equivalence for Summative Decisions. The denominator of the t-test is the standard error, which is also known as the standard deviation of the sampling distribution. The amount of variability in the sampling distribution is partly a function of sample size. Larger samples produce smaller standard errors. Thus as the number of TRF scores for a faculty member increases, the size of the standard error decreases. For very large sample sizes, the effect is to make the standard error very small. Consequently, small differences between individual faculty TRF scores and either the norm group or some criterion may be considered true differences and lead one to reject the null hypothesis. This may be problematic, and consequently I will address the problem of large sample sizes momentarily.

Another source of error to be included is measurement error, specifically, the error associated with the inability of TRF scores to perfectly measure instructor impacts on student learning and other important outcomes. The effect of this measurement error must be to increase the size of the denominator of the *t*-test and increase the size of the associated confidence interval. I therefore propose the following statistics for norm-referenced and criterion-referenced evaluation, respectively.

Norm-Based Statistical Procedure with a Correction for Measurement Error

$$t_{vc} = \frac{\overline{Y}_i - \overline{Y}_g}{\sqrt{\left(\dfrac{s_i^2}{n_i} + \dfrac{s_g^2}{n_g}\right)\left(\dfrac{1}{1 - vc}\right)}} \qquad \text{for} \quad df = n_i + n_g - 2$$

where $\overline{Y}$ is the mean TRF score, s^2 is the unbiased variance, n is sample size, vc is the validity coefficient, and df is the degrees of freedom.

In addition, one can calculate a confidence interval for the calculated value of t_{vc}:

$$CI = (\overline{Y}_i - \overline{Y}_g) \pm t_\alpha s_{Dvc}$$

where t_α is the critical value of t at a particular alpha level and

$$s_{Dvc} = \sqrt{\left(\dfrac{s_i^2}{n_i} + \dfrac{s_g^2}{n_g}\right)\left(\dfrac{1}{1 - vc}\right)}.$$

Example. Imagine the previous norm-based scenario for the faculty member's courses combined when the committee is interested in determining whether performance is worse than average (that is, a directional or one-tailed alternative hypothesis) at $p<.05$.

$$t_{vc} = \frac{4.00 - 4.17}{\sqrt{\left(\dfrac{.50^2}{200} + \dfrac{.67^2}{40{,}000}\right)\left(\dfrac{1}{1 - 0.47}\right)}} = \frac{-0.17}{.05} = -3.48.$$

This difference exceeds the critical value of -1.65.

$$CI = -0.17 \pm 1.65 \,(.05) = -0.25, -0.11 \text{ expressed as mean differences or}$$
$$3.92, 4.08 \text{ expressed as raw scores.}$$

Criterion-Based Statistical Procedures with Correction for Measurement Error

$$t_{vc} = \frac{\overline{Y}_i - C}{\sqrt{\left(\dfrac{s_i^2}{n_i}\right)\left(\dfrac{1}{1 - vc}\right)}} \qquad \text{for} \quad df = n_i - 1$$

where $\bar{Y}$ is the mean TRF score, C is the criterion score, s^2 is the unbiased variance, n is sample size, vc is the validity coefficient, and df is the degrees of freedom.

In addition, one can calculate a confidence interval for the calculated value of t:

$$CI = (\bar{Y}_i - C) \pm \underline{t}_\alpha s_C vc$$

where t_α is the critical value of t at a particular alpha level and

$$s_{Cvc} = \sqrt{\left(\frac{s_i^2}{n_i}\right)\left(\frac{1}{1 - vc}\right)}$$

Example. Imagine the previous criterion-based scenario for the faculty member's course combined when the committee is interested in determining whether performance is worse than a preset standard (a directional or one-tailed alternative hypothesis) at $p<.05$.

$$t_{vc} = \frac{4.00 - 4.15}{\sqrt{\left(\frac{.50^2}{200}\right)\left(\frac{1}{1 - 0.47}\right)}} = \frac{-0.15}{.05} = -3.00.$$

This difference exceeds the critical value of −1.65.

$$CI = -0.15 \pm 1.65 \,(.05) = -0.23, \, -0.07 \text{ expressed as mean differences or}$$
$$3.92, 4.08 \text{ expressed as raw scores.}$$

Significance. Why are such small differences still significant? The denominator of the t-test is the standard error or the standard deviation of the sampling distribution. As noted, the standard error is especially affected by sample size. When sample size is very large, the standard error is often quite small, even when the standard error is corrected for measurement error.

In the examples used to this point, I have followed what appears to be the common practice of treating students, not classes, as the units of analysis. If, however, one accepts that the unit of analysis should be the professor, then the class mean TRF score becomes the smallest data point. There are two consequences of treating the class mean as the unit of analysis: (1) the standard error will increase in size, making the confidence interval larger, and (2) it will no longer be possible to conduct tests of significance on the mean TRF score from only one class because there is only a single data point.

Note the effect of changing the unit of analysis to class means. For illustration purposes only, the average class size was assumed to be twenty students and n was adjusted accordingly. This method will yield an accurate estimate if between-class variability is approximately equal to within-class variability. Nevertheless, for accuracy, it is always preferable, albeit time-consuming, to compute variability directly from the set of class mean TRF scores.

Example. Imagine the previous norm-based scenario for the faculty member's courses combined when the committee is interested in determining whether performance is worse than average (a directional or one-tailed alternative hypothesis) at $p<.05$. Using the formula with correction for measurement error and using class means as the units of analysis yields the following:

$$t_{vc} = \frac{4.00 - 4.17}{\sqrt{\left(\dfrac{.50^2}{10} + \dfrac{.67^2}{2,000}\right)\left(\dfrac{1}{1 - 0.47}\right)}} = \frac{-0.17}{0.22} = -0.77.$$

This difference fails to exceed the critical value of -1.65.

$$CI = -0.17 \pm 1.65 \ (.22) = -0.53, +0.\ 19 \text{ expressed as mean differences or}$$
$$3.64, 4.36 \text{ expressed as raw scores.}$$

For this example, a faculty member's mean TRF scores would need to be lower than 3.80 for the committee to reach a negative decision about teaching effectiveness.

A Final Word on Sample Size. The statistical procedures I have described in this chapter are affected by sample size. All other things being equal, the larger the sample size, the smaller the differences needed to reject the null hypothesis. When students are the units of analysis, this can unwittingly create a bias in favor of instructors who have taught many courses or have taught a few courses with large enrollments. When classes are the units of analysis, this can unwittingly create a bias in favor of instructors who have taught many or large classes. For norm-based summative evaluations, in particular, it may be wise to control or equate sample sizes for all faculty. For example, when class means are the units of analysis, faculty may be asked to submit data for their ten highest-rated courses. When students are the units of analysis, the sample size used for calculating the standard error may be set uniformly for all faculty and not allowed to vary, even if this artificially reduces n in some instances.

Unwanted Variability: Systematic Versus Unsystematic Sources. A consequence of using the measure of equivalence for summative decisions is that it treats extraneous variability as unsystematic or error variability. Simply put, it means that one assumes that extraneous influences operate by chance to affect the ability of student ratings to predict an instructor's impact on student learning. This is not to suggest that the operation of these extraneous influences is not accounted for. Quite the contrary; the inclusion of the validity coefficient in the denominator of the t-test does just that.

There is ample evidence to support the reasonableness of treating extraneous influences as unsystematic sources of influence. Few, if any, extraneous factors have been identified whose influence is widely known, uniform, and of practical importance (Marsh, 1987). Extraneous factors known to influence the validity coefficient can be accounted for by adjusting upward or downward the size of the validity coefficient used in the t-ratio. Extraneous factors that influence only TRF scores (as when faculty ratings are unfairly affected by an extraneous source) call for the use of special norm groups (for example, for class size, type, or level) or the statistical upward or downward adjustment of TRF scores.

Final Recommendations

Here are nine recommendations for improving judgments about teaching effectiveness using TRFs.

1. Report the average of several global items (or a weighted average of specific items if global items are not included in the TRF).

2. Combine the results of each faculty member's courses. Decide in advance whether the mean will reflect the average rating for courses (unweighted mean) or the average rating for students (weighted mean).

3. Decide in advance on the policy for excluding TRF scores by choosing one of the following alternatives: (a) include TRFs for all courses; (b) include TRFs for all courses after they have been taught at least once; (c) include TRFs for all courses but those agreed on in advance (excluding, say, small seminars); or (d) include TRFs for the same number of courses for all faculty (for example, include the ten best-rated courses).

4. Choose between norm-referenced and criterion-referenced evaluation. If norm-referenced, select the appropriate comparison group and relative level of acceptable performance in advance. If criterion-referenced, select the absolute level of acceptable performance in advance.

5. Follow the steps in statistical hypothesis testing: (a) state the null hypothesis; (b) state the alternative hypothesis; (c) select a probability value for significance testing; (d) select the appropriate statistical test; (e) compute the calculated value; (f) determine the critical value; (g) compare the calculated and critical values in order to choose between the null and alternative hypotheses.

6. Provide descriptive and inferential statistics, and illustrate them in a visual display that shows both the point estimation and interval estimation used for statistical inference.

7. Incorporate TRF validity estimates into statistical tests and confidence intervals.

8. Because we are interested in instructor effectiveness and not student characteristics, consider using class means and not individual students as the units of analysis.

9. Decide whether and to what extent to weigh sources of evidence other than TRFs.

A Comprehensive Example

As part of their deliberations, a promotion and tenure committee is charged with determining whether the teaching at a junior colleague is of sufficient quality. The committee decides to use evidence from TRFs to reach a conclusion about teaching effectiveness, using other sources (course outlines, examinations, instructor self-assessment) as supplemental evidence concerning the faculty's efforts to teach effectively.

The university's administration, in consultation with the faculty union and the faculty development office, has set guidelines for the use of student ratings in summative decisions. The recommendation is that the promotion and tenure committees use global ratings of teaching effectiveness, allow the instructor to select the most recent ten courses for analysis, use class means as the units of analysis, and conclude that teaching is acceptable if an instructor's ratings are not significantly ($p<.05$) worse than the lowest third of all instructors in the faculty.

The committee asks the faculty development office to provide the results after the instructor selects ten courses for analysis. The relevant descriptive and inferential statistics are as follows:

TRF Descriptive Statistics

Source	Instructor	Faculty (33%ile)
Mean global ratings	3.50	3.80
Standard deviation	0.55	0.60
Sample size (courses)	10	1,000

TRF Inferential Statistics

H_0: μ_1 = 33%ile
H_a: μ_1 < 33%ile
$p <.05$

$$t_{vc} = \frac{\bar{Y}_i - \bar{Y}_g}{\sqrt{\left(\frac{s_i^2}{n_i} + \frac{s_g^2}{n_g}\right)\left(\frac{1}{1 - vc}\right)}} \quad \text{for} \quad df = n_i + n_g - 2$$

$$CI = (\bar{Y}_i - \bar{Y}_g) \pm t_\alpha s_{Dvc}$$

$$t_{vc} = \frac{3.50 - 3.80}{\sqrt{\left(\frac{.55^2}{10} + \frac{.60^2}{1,000}\right)\left(\frac{1}{1 - 0.47}\right)}} = \frac{-0.30}{0.24} = -1.25$$

$CI = -0.30 \pm 1.65 (.24) = -0.70, +0.10$ expressed as mean differences or
3.10, 3.90 expressed as raw scores.

The calculated *t*-value difference fails to exceed the critical value of –1.65. There is therefore insufficient evidence to conclude that the faculty member's teaching is inferior to the 33rd percentile teaching performance of instructors in the faculty.

Visual Display

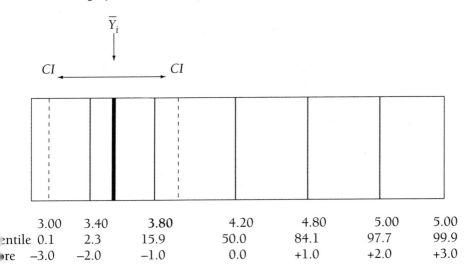

	3.00	3.40	**3.80**	4.20	4.80	5.00	5.00
entile	0.1	2.3	15.9	50.0	84.1	97.7	99.9
re	–3.0	–2.0	–1.0	0.0	+1.0	+2.0	+3.0

The dark, solid line shows the combined mean TRF score for the faculty member. The dashed lines represents the confidence interval surrounding the significance test of mean differences. The visual display shows that the faculty member has insignificantly lower TRF scores than the norm group. The 95 percent confidence interval (3.10 to 3.90 in raw scores) in which the mean TRF score lies includes the 33rd percentile of the comparison group (3.80 in raw scores). In other words, the analysis of student ratings in this case supports a conclusion that teaching is acceptable.

References

Abrami, P. C. "Using Student Rating Norm Groups for Summative Evaluation." *Faculty Evaluation and Development,* 1993, *13,* 5–9.

Abrami, P. C., d'Apollonia, S., and Rosenfield, S. "The Dimensionality of Student Ratings of Instruction: What We Know and What We Do Not." In R. P. Perry and J. C. Smart (eds.), *Effective Teaching in Higher Education: Research and Practice.* New York: Agathon Press, 1996.

Abrami, P. C., Dickens, W. J., Perry, R. P., and Leventhal, L. "Do Teacher Standards for Assigning Grades Affect Student Evaluations of Instruction?" *Journal of Educational Psychology,* 1980, *72,* 107–118.

Abrami, P. C., Leventhal, L., and Perry, R. P. "Educational Seduction." *Review of Educational Research,* 1982, *52,* 446–464.

Aleamoni, L. M. "Why We Do Need Norms of Student Ratings to Evaluate Faculty: Reaction to McKeachie." *Instructional Evaluation and Faculty Development,* 1996, *15*(1–2), 18–19.

Canadian Association of University Teachers, Academic Freedom and Tenure Committee. *Policy on the Use of Anonymous Student Questionnaires in the Evaluation of Teaching.* Ottawa: Canadian Association of University Teachers, 1998.

Cashin, W. E. "Student Ratings: The Need for Comparative Data." *Instructional Evaluation and Faculty Development,* 1992, *12*(2), 1–6.

Cashin, W. E. "Student Ratings: Comparative Data, Norm Groups, and Non-Comparative Interpretations: Reply to Hativa and to Abrami." *Instructional Evaluation and Faculty Development,* 1994, *14*(1–2), 21–26.

Cashin, W. E. "Should Student Ratings Be Interpreted Absolutely or Relatively? Reaction to McKeachie." *Instructional Evaluation and Faculty Development,* 1996, *16*(2), 14–19.

Cashin, P.A. "Skewed Student Ratings and Parametrtic Statistics: A Query." *Instructional Evaluation and Faculty Development,* 1998, *17*(1), 3–8.

Cohen, P. A. "Student Ratings of Instruction and Student Achievement: A Meta-Analysis of Multisection Validity Studies." *Review of Educational Research,* 1981, *51,* 281–309.

Crumbley, L. "Society for a Return to Academic Standards Web Site." [http://www.bus.lsu.edu/accounting/faculty/lcrumbley/sfrtas.html]. 1996.

Damron, J. C. "Politics of the Classroom." [http://vax1.mankato.msus.edu/~pkbrando/damron_politics.html]. 1996.

d'Apollonia, S., and Abrami, P. C. "Variables Moderating the Validity of Student Ratings of Instruction: A Meta-Analysis." Paper presented at the 77th Annual Meeting of the American Educational Research Association, New York, Apr. 1996.

d'Apollonia, S., and Abrami, P. C. "Scaling the Ivory Tower, Part 1: Collecting Evidence of Instructor Effectiveness." *Psychology Teaching Review,* 1997a, *6,* 46–59.

d'Apollonia, S., and Abrami, P. C. "Scaling the Ivory Tower, Part 2: Student Ratings of Instruction in North America." *Psychology Teaching Review,* 1997b, *6,* 60–76.

d'Apollonia, S., and Abrami, P. C. "In Response." *Change,* 1997c, *29*(5), 18–19.

d'Apollonia, S., Lou, Y., and Abrami, P. C. "Making the Grade: A Meta-Analysis on the Influence of Grade Inflation on Student Ratings." Paper presented at the 79th Annual Meeting of the American Educational Research Association, San Diego, Apr. 1998.

Feldman, K. A. "Consistency and Variability Among College Students in Rating Their Teachers and Courses: A Review and Analysis." *Research in Higher Education,* 1977, *6,* 223–274.

Feldman, K. A. "The Association Between Student Ratings of Specific Instructional Dimensions and Student Achievement: Refining and Extending the Synthesis of Data from Multisection Validity Studies." *Research in Higher Education,* 1989, *30,* 583–645.

Feldman, K. A. "An Afterword for 'The Association Between Student Ratings of Specific Instructional Dimensions and Student Achievement: Refining and Extending the Synthesis of Data from Multisection Validity Studies." *Research in Higher Education,* 1990, *31,* 315–318.

Greenwald, A. G., and Gillmore, G. M. "Grading Leniency Is a Removable Contaminant of Student Ratings." *American Psychologist,* 1997a, *52,* 1209–1217.

Greenwald, A. G., and Gillmore, G. M. "No Pain, No Gain? The Importance of Measuring Course Workload in Student Ratings of Instruction." *Journal of Educational Psychology,* 1997b, *89,* 743–751.

Haskell, R. E. "Academic Freedom, Tenure, and Student Evaluation of Faculty: Galloping Polls in the 21st Century." *Education Policy Analysis Archives,* 1997, *5*(6). [http://olam.ed.asu.edu/epaa/v5n6.html].

Hativa, N. "Student Ratings: A Non-Comparative Interpretation." *Instructional Evaluation and Faculty Development,* 1993, *13*(2), 1–4.

Marsh, H. W. "Students' Evaluations of University Teaching: Research Findings, Methodological Issues, and Directions for Future Research." *International Journal of Educational Research,* 1987, *11,* 253–388.

Marsh, H. W., and Roche, L. A. "Effects of Grading Leniency and Low Workloads on Students' Evaluations of Teaching: Popular Myth, Bias, Validity, or Innocent Bystanders?" Paper presented at the 79th Annual Meeting of the American Educational Research Association, San Diego, Calif., Apr. 1998.

McKeachie, W. J. "Do We Need Norms of Student Ratings to Evaluate Faculty?" *Instructional Evaluation and Faculty Development*, 1996, *15*(1–2), 14–17.

Naftulin, D. H., Ware, J. E., and Donnelly, F. A. "The Doctor Fox Lecture: A Paradigm of Educational Seduction." *Journal of Medical Education*, 1973, *48*, 630–635.

Theall, M. "Who Is Norm, and What Does He Have to Do with Student Ratings? A Reaction to McKeachie." *Instructional Evaluation and Faculty Development*, 1996, *16*(1), 7–9.

Williams, W. M., and Ceci, S. J. "How'm I Doing? Problems with Student Ratings of Instructors and Courses." *Change*, 1997, *29*(5), 13–23.

PHILIP C. ABRAMI is professor and director of the Centre for the Study of Learning and Performance at Concordia University, Montreal, Quebec, Canada.

Evaluation researchers and practitioners agree that although measurement issues remain important to good evaluation practice, a greater area of concern is unreliable or invalid day-to-day practice. Can the precision of statistical techniques be brought to bear on this problem?

5

Can We Put Precision into Practice? Commentary and Thoughts Engendered by Abrami's "Improving Judgments About Teaching Effectiveness Using Teacher Rating Forms"

Michael Theall

Portions of Philip Abrami's Chapter Four were first presented as an invited address at the 1998 annual meeting of the American Education Research Association (AERA) in conjunction with his receipt of the Wilbert J. McKeachie Career Achievement Award presented by the AERA Special Interest Group in Faculty Teaching, Evaluation, and Development (SIGFTED).

Subsequent to the meeting, a draft of the paper was made available on the SIGFTED Web site (http://www.uis.edu/~ctl/sigfed.html) and an invitation was issued to members of SIGFTED, the Professional and Organizational Development Network, and others to comment on Abrami's proposal to use hypothesis testing as a measure of the import and implications of ratings results and a way to make better evaluative decisions. Several comments ensued, most brief and addressing specific issues rather than offering overall critiques of the paper. In this brief chapter, I will reconstruct the thrust of these comments and add my own thoughts. Abrami will then respond to the commentary in Chapter Six. It is our hope that this unique opportunity for dialogue will enhance this issue of *New Directions for Institutional Research*, heighten interest in effective evaluation practice, and perhaps lead to more discussion about the ways in which evaluation and especially ratings data can be effectively used.

Comments on Abrami

Comments in reaction to the paper on which Chapter Four is based were of two types: those dealing with statistical, measurement, or report production issues and those dealing with the applicability and usefulness of Abrami's process in higher education settings. Let us look at a sampling of the comments.

Technical Issues. Some individuals commented on technical issues. Orlando Olivares[1] (Aug. 31, 1998) noted such matters as the variance in uneven-sized samples in norm-based calculations, the correction for measurement error, and the importance of including information about effect size in ratings results. He also suggested that prior subject interest and other researched variables should have received more stress in Abrami's discussion of the literature. Although uneven-sized samples occasionally pose problems, the major statistical analysis packages contain appropriate tests that can provide estimates of such effects. Of more importance may be the sizes of the individual samples used: in evaluation, this means the enrollments of the individual classes and the ratio of students enrolled to students responding to the evaluation questionnaire. The question, especially with smaller classes (with fewer than twenty students) is whether comparisons are appropriate in any case. A typical sample size recommendation (Theall and Franklin, 1991, p. 89) for accurate interpretation of evaluation results from small classes is an enrolled-to-responded ratio of 80 percent or higher.

Olivares also noted the need for correction of measurement error and the importance of including effect size information. The quality (validity) of the instrument used is, of course, critical to accurate measurement, but the estimation of measurement error and the calculation of effect size are both closely tied to sample size. Menges and L'Hommedieu (1992), in a discussion of the investigation of the effects of feedback from course evaluations, noted three design and analysis problems that parallel Olivares's concerns: low statistical power, questionable operationalization of the treatment, and faulty implementation of the treatment. The "treatment" there was an instructional intervention, but the caution addressed the same issue, a question of precision of measurement as influenced by the nature of the sample and the conditions that may have influenced it and the appropriate interpretation of results. Menges and L'Hommedieu suggest minimum sample sizes of thirty and even characterize this estimate as too conservative. They offer calculations demonstrating that a typical class size of twenty-six, the mean class size in the studies they reviewed, "drops the power of the test to below .20; that is, 80 percent of the samples pulled from the population will fail to show an effect" (p. 19). While their focus is on studies of the effect of feedback, Olivares's caution for establishing statistical precision in the analysis and interpretation of ratings echoes this appropriate concern and asks Abrami to ensure the rigor of the procedures used.

Gerald Gillmore (July 30, 1998) asked about Abrami's process for combining data from several classes, suggesting that this might confound within-class and between-class variance. Situational and contextual differences (for example, disciplinary differences and class size) make this a reasonable proposal when dealing with individual course or instructor ratings or comparisons for summative purposes. For example, an instructor might be quite successful in graduate seminars but dramatically less successful with undergraduates in survey courses. The differences could result from teaching style and method, class sizes, students' prior preparation and interest, content density, or other factors, but the result would be to homogenize ratings results to the point where only "average" performance by this instructor is indicated. Although this might be quantitatively correct, the purpose of the ratings might be better served if strengths and weaknesses were identified. It has been the case, however, that much of the research on ratings has used large databases in attempts to generalize to larger populations, a problem discussed earlier by Feldman (1995) and myself (Theall, 1996a).

Gillmore's two major concerns with Abrami's work were, first, that a system that uses hypothesis testing and confidence intervals for reporting evaluation data can result in a false sense of precision, leading to rigid but not necessarily appropriate cutoff points for decision making, and second, that the suggestion to add 25 percent to the error band in reports to account for variance in student learning does not accomplish what Abrami intended—namely, taking into account the variance in student learning not accounted for by ratings. Gillmore's comment is similar to that of John Ory (Aug. 31, 1998), who proposed that ratings are effective as tools for identifying the top and the bottom 20 percent of the population of faculty but not very precise at determining the positions of the remaining 60 percent. Paraphrased, the question is whether the precision suggested by Abrami has social and educational significance.

Wilbert McKeachie (Aug. 6, 1998) indicated a preference for Bayesian approaches over hypothesis testing because this might make evaluation reports and use of the data more simple, especially for nonstatisticians. Although simplicity has many virtues, the question remains whether making the decision too simple denies the complexity of the issue. Hays (1973) notes that using Bayesian methods in a decision-theoretic approach to hypothesis testing requires an estimate of the loss ratio (R). In other words, if there are no relative weights given to Type I and Type II errors, what are the consequences of making either type of error? In the matter of a promotion or tenure decision, the real consequences can be significant indeed. Individuals who make decisions and those about whom decisions are made should be aware of this and should be willing to take the risks of making either type of error. McKeachie also noted a preference for visual displays such as those Abrami proposes. Further support for visual displays came from Jennifer Franklin (Aug. 27, 1998), who noted that she had successfully field-tested and had been using a visual display component based on confidence intervals at a large private eastern university since the late 1980s. Though visual displays can clearly identify individuals above or below the confidence intervals, their greater value perhaps lies in that they also clearly show overlaps of the intervals and signal when a simple yes-no decision cannot be made on the basis of the data.

William Cashin (Aug. 27, 1998) raised several technical issues having to do with interpretation of results. He noted the skewness typical of ratings data and pointed out that when norm groups have high ratings, the opportunity for individual instructors to achieve significantly higher ratings is reduced. He acknowledged the recent discussion of "grade inflation" (Gillmore and others, 1998) but expressed the opinion that if a student gets a higher grade than usual in a given course, that higher grade probably indicates greater learning. He also pointed out that on occasion, students get high grades "because they learned much, but on their own *despite* the instructor" (emphasis in the original). In a comment about the meaning of "true scores," Cashin expressed concern that some readers may overinterpret the term and presume such scores to be constant. His view was that teaching effectiveness scores can change over time. Finally, Cashin felt that more stress should be put on the use of class means as the unit of analysis because the emphasis of ratings should be on the instructor's characteristics rather than the students'. Cashin's comments suggest caution in the presentation of ratings results primarily to promote more accurate interpretation of the data. He did not take exception to Abrami's proposed procedures, indicating that they provide a useful and explicit set of decision rules.

In sum, the comments about technical issues address specific points, which seem to be minor matters of calculation when considered in light of concerns about the interpretation and use of even precise data. Abrami will deal with these or other technical issues in his response.

Real-World Applications. "Real-world applications" constituted a larger area for discussion. Comments here went beyond Abrami's specific proposals and had to do with evaluation practices. The thrust of comments in this area was to question whether Abrami's proposal was feasible in day-to-day practice. The comments did not question the rigor or appropriateness of the process Abrami recommended. In fact, there was general agreement that the paper was scholarly and the proposals quite rigorous. Rather, the issue was whether hypothesis testing was too complex or difficult or time-consuming for use by sometimes untrained decision makers and whether the precision of measurement it provided would result in better evaluation. Raoul Arreola and Lawrence Aleamoni (Sept. 3, 1998) phrased this as follows: "The assumption that we question is that a measurement constitutes an evaluation and that, somehow, evaluations can be made more objective. . . . If we take Abrami's paper as dealing exclusively with the measurement of teaching, then it constitutes a valuable professional contribution. However, we should be careful not to confuse measurement with evaluation."

William Cashin (Aug. 27, 1998) raised questions about institutional interest in teaching and the extent to which teaching "counts," noting that "in summative evaluation, we want to make decisions about the instructor's *general* teaching ability . . . to generalize to the instructor's *future,* therefore general, teaching ability" (emphasis in the original). Cashin also questioned the equivalence of teacher rating forms and achievement, suggesting that achievement is controlled largely by students whereas teaching is largely under the instructor's control. This suggests that even given the established relationship of ratings to learning (Cohen, 1981), the question of the instructor's responsibility for student learning must be more clearly framed and the determined responsibility better defined and described.

Katherine Ryan (Aug. 31, 1998) asked four questions bearing on evaluation in general and on the application of Abrami's proposal. The first was whether a shared and clearly understood definition of judgment is or would be applied when evaluation decisions are made. The second question addressed the potential positive and negative effects of using hypothesis testing in evaluation. The third and fourth questions essentially proposed that any empirical approach to decision making should be supported by the use of other data from multiple sources. These questions could be summarized as expressing concern that the precision of statistical testing might create the impression that other data were unnecessary. This view mirrors the consensus among evaluation researchers and writers (for example, Arreola, 1994) that multiple data sources and formats are not merely recommended but required for accurate evaluation. In a related but more specific opinion, John Ory (Aug. 31, 1998) expressed concern about administrators and others who rely on student ratings "as *the* measure of teaching effectiveness" (emphasis in the original), going on to propose that hypothesis testing was inappropriate for summative purposes because "student ratings are very effective measures for identifying the top 20 percent and the bottom 20 percent of instructors and nothing more" and adding, "We need to use our imagination and resources . . . to help sift through the middle 60 percent."

These comments lead to the issue of the use of data in everyday decision making and the skills and knowledge of those who use the data. As Jennifer Franklin and I noted in Chapter Three of this volume and in an earlier work (Franklin and Theall, 1989), we are also concerned about the knowledge, attitudes, and practices of those who use ratings data. Our research has revealed a surprising and disturbing lack of knowledge among faculty and administrator users of ratings data and a significant correlation between lack of knowledge and negative attitudes about evaluation, students as providers of data, and student ratings in general. More recently, the *Chronicle of Higher Education* set up an electronic "colloquy" forum wherein fifty-eight individuals responded to a feature article by Robin Wilson (1998). The article discussed recent studies of student ratings and questioned whether ratings were valid indicators of teaching performance. In my review of these comments (Theall, 1998), I concluded that the ratio of negative and uninformed comments to comments indicating knowledge of the literature was greater than five to one. Research by Centra (1993) and Robinson (1993) suggests that faculty even have problems making accurate decisions based on nonquantitative data and are not comfortable with their ability to use these data accurately or effectively. The lack of user knowledge reinforces the concern of the many who noted that increasing the level of precision of the reported data might lead to even greater overreliance on ratings as the sole data source for summative decision making. Part of the solution to these kinds of problems is to develop a comprehensive system for faculty evaluation (Arreola, 1994) that begins with definition and clarification of the issues and areas ("components") to be evaluated and follows with consensus about the weight assigned to each component and the determination about the choices of data sources and their respective levels of input. In essence, a complete system provides structure and guidelines for decision making, builds in appropriate formats for reporting data, and includes specific explanations and instructions for those who interpret and use the data. Jennifer Franklin and I have presented a similar argument (Franklin and Theall, 1990).

Summary

The comments and questions about Abrami's proposal reflect the growing concern among evaluation researchers that questions about bias in ratings must extend beyond issues relating to students alone and into the contexts of evaluation and evaluation practice itself (for example, Feldman, 1995; Theall, 1996a). Indeed, the biases of the users of ratings data may be of far greater concern than those of students, and the frequency of poor practice (such as the increasing reliance on ratings as shown by Seldin, 1984, in his series of works on evaluation practice) indicates that more widespread evaluation does not necessarily mean better evaluation. Thus there is ample evidence that the expressed concerns are not purely theoretical.

Abrami's proposal brings the rigorous application of statistical techniques to the analysis and reporting of student ratings data. The question is whether such rigor is sufficient to influence practice in positive directions. I fear it will not, but I will not discount the possibility that it can, because I also believe that increased precision is necessary and that we must continue to explore new and more accurate ways of dealing with ratings and other evaluation data. For example, Jennifer Franklin and I have found that the use of graphic displays without accompanying mean scores draws the attention of users of the data to the overlap of confidence intervals when such occurs. Accompanying guidelines for interpretation of the data stress that when confidence intervals overlap, one cannot conclude that there is a significant difference in the scores represented and therefore one cannot say that one individual is "better" or "worse" than the comparison group. This is not to say that mean scores or other bases for comparisons are inappropriate, but this subject has also been raised. In a commentary in *Instructional Evaluation and Faculty Development,* McKeachie (1996) questioned the use of norms in student ratings, concluding that norms are more often misused than helpful. Others (Aleamoni, 1996; Cashin, 1997; Theall 1996b) conceded that misuse occurs but argued that some basis for comparison must exist and that no better statistic than the mean has yet been offered.

One of the key points in Abrami's presentation is that there is an established, significant, and meaningful relationship between ratings and learning and because of this, precision in the presentation of information about ratings results is important, necessary, and useful. Cohen's work (1981) and Abrami's meta-analytic reviews (for example, Abrami and d'Apollonia, 1987; d'Apollonia and Abrami, 1987) support this argument. Others (Greenwald and Gillmore, 1997) suggest that alternative hypotheses can be presented to account for variance in ratings and that presentation of ratings results must take these factors into account. If one accepts this proposition, the inescapable conclusion is that if other factors do influence ratings, then even the most precise calculations of ratings results cannot be assumed to indicate the quality of teaching directly or fully. Therein lies a major issue.

In paraphrase, we might state this concern as follows: We know that we are accurately and precisely measuring something, but is it purely the quality of teaching that we are measuring? In cases where good, effective teaching leads to learning (or in the polar opposite, where teaching is very poor and little learning results), I would venture that the answer is yes. In those cases (the majority, unfortunately) where the indicators are not so clear, I would optimistically say that the answer is probably. However, we must be careful to keep in mind that teaching is not purely a science. It is a complex, multidimensional, dynamic process that defies perfect description. When we attempt to measure the quality of teaching, we must use all the available tools and we must know what we are looking for and what we value. We in the field of faculty evaluation must continue to stress and argue for improvement of overall practice. This means better theory, better research, and better measurement as we strive for the most accurate and most interpretable data that we can gather and present to decision makers. With his paper and Chapter Four of this volume, Abrami has helped us move in that direction

Note

1. All comments reported in this chapter were submitted as personal e-mail messages or as postings to the SIGFED listserv. The date of their sending or posting is given in parentheses.

References

Abrami, P. C., and d'Apollonia, S. "A Conceptual Critique of Meta-Analysis: The Literature on Student Ratings." Paper presented at the 68th Annual Meeting of the American Educational Research Association, Washington, D.C., Apr. 1987.
Aleamoni, L. M. "Why We Do Need Norms of Student Ratings to Evaluate Faculty: Reaction to McKeachie." *Instructional Evaluation and Faculty Development*, 1996, 15(1–2), 18–19.
Arreola, R. A. *Developing a Comprehensive Faculty Evaluation System*. Boston: Anker, 1994.
Cashin, W. E. "Should Student Ratings Be Interpreted Absolutely or Relatively? Reaction to McKeachie." *Instructional Evaluation and Faculty Development*. 1997, 16(2), 14–19.

Centra, J. A. *The Use of Teaching Portfolios for Summative Evaluation.* Paper presented at the 74th Annual Meeting of the American Educational Research Association, Atlanta, Apr. 1993.

Cohen, P. A. "Student Ratings of Instruction and Student Achievement: A Meta-Analysis of Multisection Validity Studies." *Review of Educational Research,* 1981, *51,* 281–309.

d'Apollonia, S. and Abrami, P. C. "An Empirical Critique of Meta-Analysis: The Literature on Student Ratings." Paper presented at the 68th Annual Meeting of the American Educational Research Association, Washington, D. C., Apr. 1987.

Feldman, K. A. "Some Unresolved Issues in Studying Instructional Effectiveness in Student Ratings." Address delivered at the 76th Annual Meeting of the American Educational Research Association, San Francisco, Apr. 1995.

Franklin, J. L., and Theall, M. "Who Reads Ratings: Knowledge, Attitudes, and Practice of Users of Student Ratings of Instruction." Paper presented at the 70th Annual Meeting of the American Educational Research Association, San Francisco, Mar. 1989.

Franklin, J. L., and Theall, M. "Communicating Ratings Results to Decision Makers: Design for Good Practice." In M. Theall and J. L. Franklin (eds.), *Student Ratings of Instruction: Issues for Improving Practice.* New Directions for Teaching and Learning, no. 43. San Francisco: Jossey Bass, 1990.

Gillmore, G. M., and others. "The Positive Relationship Between Course Grades and Course Ratings: What Is the Cause, and What, If Anything, Should Be Done About It?" Debate presented at the 79th Annual Meeting of the American Educational Research Association, San Diego, Apr. 1998.

Greenwald, A. G., and Gillmore, G. M. "Grading Leniency Is a Removable Contaminant of Student Ratings." *American Psychologist,* 1997, *52,* 1209–1217.

Hays, W. L. *Statistics for the Social Sciences.* (2nd ed.) Austin, Tex.: Holt, Rinehart and Winston, 1973.

McKeachie, W. J. "Do We Need Norms of Student Ratings to Evaluate Faculty?" *Instructional Evaluation and Faculty Development,* 1996, *15*(1–2), 14–17.

Menges, R. J., and L'Hommedieu, R. "Toward More Conclusive Studies of Student Ratings Feedback." *Instructional Evaluation and Faculty Development,* 1992, *12*(2), 17–23.

Robinson, J. E. "Faculty Orientations Toward Teaching and the Use of Teaching Portfolios for Evaluating and Improving University-Level Instruction." Paper presented at the 74th Annual Meeting of the American Educational Research Association. Atlanta, Apr. 1993.

Seldin, P. *Changing Practices in Faculty Evaluation: A Critical Assessment and Recommendations for Improvement.* San Francisco: Jossey-Bass, 1984.

Theall, M. "When Meta-Analysis Isn't Enough: A Report of a Symposium About Student Ratings, Conflicting Results, and Issues That Won't Go Away." *Instructional Evaluation and Faculty Development,* 1996a, *15*(1–2), 1–14.

Theall, M. "Who Is Norm, and What Does He Have to Do with Student Ratings? A Reaction to McKeachie." *Instructional Evaluation and Faculty Development,* 1996b, *16*(1), 7–9.

Theall, M. "Colloquy, Colloquia, Colloquiarum: A Declining Form, a Questionable Forum." *Instructional Evaluation and Faculty Development,* 1998, *18*(1–2), http://www.uis.edu/ctl/sigfted.html.

Theall, M., and Franklin, J. L. "Using Student Ratings for Teaching Improvement." In M. Theall and J. L. Franklin (eds.), *Effective Practices for Improving Teaching.* New Directions for Teaching and Learning, no. 48. San Francisco: Jossey Bass, 1991.

Wilson, R. "New Research Casts Doubt on Value of Student Evaluations of Professors." *Chronicle of Higher Education,* Jan. 16, 1998, pp. A1, A16.

MICHAEL THEALL is associate professor of educational administration and director of the Center for Teaching and Learning at the University of Illinois at Springfield.

6

This rejoinder is organized around two themes: statistical and measurement issues and applicability and usefulness issues. The author concludes that his earlier suggestions for improving judgments about teaching effectiveness can accomplish their objectives.

Improving Judgments About Teaching Effectiveness: How to Lie Without Statistics

Philip C. Abrami

I would like to begin this rejoinder by thanking both those colleagues who provided feedback on my paper, which became the basis for Chapter Four of this volume, and Mike Theall for volunteering to summarize the comments as well as add his own in Chapter Five. This has been an interesting and unique exercise and one that bears repeating, especially if the end result is the advancement of knowledge and the improvement of the practice of instructional evaluation.

Theall organized his reply around two major themes: statistical and measurement issues and applicability and usefulness issues. I will use the same themes in presenting my response.

Statistical and Measurement Issues

My main purpose in proposing statistical procedures with a correction for the size of the validity coefficient was to recognize mathematically that teacher rating forms (TRFs) do not provide perfect estimates of instructor impacts on student learning and other criteria of effective teaching. These procedures were based on two other premises.

First, although imprecision is widely known among researchers, as well as administrators and instructors, it remains my contention that the degree of the imprecision is not always accounted for in practice. Some summative decisions about instructional effectiveness are improperly lenient and some decisions are improperly strict. Either type of decision error, when it is based on the misinterpretation of TRF scores, should be

New Directions for Institutional Research, no. 109, Spring 2001   © Jossey-Bass, A Publishing Unit of John Wiley & Sons, Inc.

avoided, in my opinion. My recommendations attempt to provide tools for minimizing the misinterpretation of TRF scores and improve current practice. Note that Theall also raised concerns about "a surprising and disturbing lack of knowledge among faculty and administrator users of ratings data."

Second, there are a host of factors that may contribute to the inability of TRF scores to explain completely the variability in instructor impacts on student learning. In general, these unwanted sources of variability or influence appear not to operate uniformly or consistently. In addition, these unwanted sources of variability may be correlated with desirable sources of influence.

The recent renewal of the controversy over instructor grading standards and TRF scores is a useful illustration of my concern. For example, Greenwald and Gillmore (1997) would have us believe that lenient grading standards encourage students to assign higher TRF scores even though learning may not be enhanced. One potential implication of this contention for summative evaluations would be to systematically adjust ratings downward after the fact for instructors who assign high grades.

The conclusions from meta-analysis of the grades-rating literature conducted by my colleagues and me (d'Apollonia, Lou, and Abrami, 1998) speak against such an adjustment. We found that the influence of grading standards was small on average, variable, and not necessarily independent of the desirable influences of instructors on ratings and student learning. Some instructors may be assigned even worse ratings when they attempt to use high grades to influence TRF scores. In addition, students who receive high grades may deserve them, and consequently, the instructors who teach them may also deserve high TRF scores. Therefore, the implication of our review was to avoid systematically adjusting all ratings downward when instructors assign high grades.

The grades-rating issue represents one of several examples of the problem of treating unwanted variability in TRF scores as systematic variability, which can be controlled by adjusting ratings upward or downward statistically. TRF scores are not perfect predictors, and teaching and learning contexts are far too variable and complex for us to say with certainty whether and how to control extraneous influences systematically. It is also the case that if these sorts of uniform adjustments are not advisable statistically, there is less wisdom in attempting them by committee guesswork. Importantly, my application of a correction for the size of the validity coefficient recognizes that this imprecision exists and that many extraneous influences operate in an irregular or inconsistent fashion. Sometimes these extraneous influences may incorrectly raise TRF scores and sometimes incorrectly lower them. The correction for the size of the validity coefficient recognizes that either type of influence may operate. And the statistical test asks the following type of question: Are a faculty member's ratings different enough from the criterion (or normative) score that we can be reasonably certain that the difference reflects more than the operation of (a large amount of) unsystematic variation in TRF scores?

Otherwise, I like the suggestion of augmenting the adjusted statistical test with estimates of effect size and power. We may want to know not only whether a difference is statistically significant but also the magnitude of that difference. If effect size estimates were to be computed in addition to the statistical test, they should be based on difference scores in the numerator and validity coefficient–adjusted standard deviations in the numerator. Computing the power of each adjusted statistical test may also serve as a warning of low sample sizes or excessive variability when differences are too small to be judged significant. Issues of statistical power may arise on occasion if my recommendation is followed to use class means as the units of analysis.

I am less certain of the viability of using Bayesian approaches to statistical inference compared to the classic Fisherian methods I recommended. Perhaps someone will develop this idea further and illustrate how it might also be used to improve the summative decision process.

Pooled and separate variance model t-tests with adjusted degrees of freedom may be employed, depending on the degree of variance and sample size heterogeneity. Furthermore, I did not intend to confuse within-class and between-class variability but used the former as a convenient substitute for the latter in my sample calculations only. When class means are the units of analysis, I noted, "it is always preferable, albeit time-consuming, to compute variability directly from the set of class mean TRF scores."

Finally, I suggested an aggregation of student ratings from multiple classes because promotion and tenure committees need to reach decisions about teaching effectiveness in general. Nevertheless, the procedures I recommended also account for or report between-class variability on TRF scores (standard deviation, statistical test, and visual-display). An instructor whose class mean ratings are variable will have a larger standard deviation, a smaller calculated value, and a larger confidence interval. Otherwise, subsets of class mean ratings may be examined separately or weighted differently to the extent it is logical and ethical to do so in summative decisions.

Applicability and Usefulness Issues

I am puzzled by some of the concerns raised about the applicability and usefulness of the suggestions I offered for improving judgments of teaching effectiveness using TRFs. First, I am puzzled not only because these concerns do not refute my claim that the use of TRFs for summative decisions needs improvement but also because the individuals who voiced the concerns offered no concrete suggestions for improvement. Because I find that the status quo needs improvement, I made numerous recommendations for change. Am I wrong? If so, what are some concrete alternatives to my recommendations? Second, I am puzzled because I offered a number of suggestions that are quite easy to implement; not every suggestion hinged on using inferential statistical procedures. What about these other recommendations?

Third, I am puzzled because it is rather difficult to reject as impracticable something that has never been tried. Consequently, I invite faculty developers to try my ideas first and then report on their findings.

My suggestions regarding the use of TRF scores to improve judgments about teaching effectiveness should not be construed as a recommendation that student ratings are the only source of evidence on effective teaching. I stated quite baldly: "Other evidence of teaching effectiveness should also be used in making summative decisions." It remains to be determined how the recommendations I developed for student ratings can be expanded to include other sources of evidence.

Let me reply in more detail to concerns about practicality. First, I believe that the summary statistics, visual display, and single statistical test I suggested are quite easy for a university professor to read and interpret. Second, I did not for a moment think it was going to be that same professor who prepared the summary statistics, visual display, and single statistical summary. I assumed that the standard practice of having these results prepared by the faculty development office or university computer center would continue.

I use many highly complex and sophisticated tools in my professional and personal life. Like most people, I drive a car, watch television, and use a personal computer. I understand how to use these tools but haven't a clue how to design, build, or repair them. They are sophisticated devices that are nevertheless easy to use.

I have saved what appears to be the most common concern for last. My suggestion to use a statistical test adjusted by the size of the validity coefficient to help improve summative decisions about teaching effectiveness drew several negative reactions.

One thread to these concerns was that the statistical procedures I proposed would mechanize the evaluation process and disallow or discredit human judgment. I will admit that a degree of this criticism is true. As I noted in the introduction to my proposal, I contend that tenure and promotion committees are ill equipped to handle the mass of evaluation data provided to them. Because there is little, if any, guidance on assembling and interpreting these data, mistakes in judgment are made.

I provided clear guidelines for assembling these data in ways that both simplify the evaluation process and prevent both inconsistent procedures and incorrect procedures from subverting good judgment. I also recognized that many people regard both contextual effects and selectivity as important, as I once did. "Twenty years ago, I would have argued against my own recommendations," I wrote. ". . . Time, unfortunately, has proved my initial position wrong."

Let me expand on this thinking and correct an imprecision on my part. I do not wish to argue that contextual and idiosyncratic influences on TRF scores do not occur. Quite the contrary. I have argued in Chapter Four and here that there are few, if any, systematic, uniform extraneous influences on TRF scores. The influence of these extraneous influences is instead unsystematic, highly idiosyncratic, and context-specific. Indeed, the very heart of the statistical adjustment I suggested tackles this problem head on. It requires promotion and tenure committees to recognize that student ratings predict only modestly the extent to which instructors affect student learning.

We have known this for some time, but errors in judgment occur. My hope is that if we change the way the evidence is reported, judgments will improve. Allowing a promotion and tenure committee to assemble and weigh the evidence suggests that committee members are both knowledge-able of the literature and able to decide the extent to which contextual and idiosyncratic influences operate. I think this is an extremely tenuous argument.

It is my thesis that if we provide promotion and tenure committees with evidence that takes into account the general influence of extraneous influences, more correct decisions will be reached. And I'd be happy if someone would put this to the test.

Finally, providing clear data and interpretative guidelines does not mean that human judgment is ignored. Promotion and tenure committees may elect to confirm what the statistical tests reveal or disconfirm them. Here, too, it is my intention that if the statistical findings are rejected, a reasoned argument should be provided. That reasoned argument would need to make a cogent case why extraneous influences were either much greater than the statistical procedure accounts for or much smaller. That sounds pretty reasonable to me.

I subtitled this rejoinder "How to Lie Without Statistics" to emphasize that the wise and correct use of statistical tools and procedures can go a long way toward overcoming the (covert and overt) forms of bias that characterize uneducated subjective judgment. Though I concentrated on quantitative procedures in my solution, other procedures, including qualitative ones, may also be viable. In either case, we must research ways to encourage better judgments of teaching effectiveness than current practice. Failing to do so may diminish the recognition offered to good teaching in postsecondary education.

The last argument I wish to address concerns the misplaced precision of statistical tests. I find this argument ironic when applied to the statistical test I recommended. Using the validity coefficient to adjust the denominator of the test statistic decreases the power and precision of the test. It takes into account additional extraneous influences and adds them to error variability. Consequently, it is as wrong to call the statistical test I recommend overly precise as it is wrong to call the test too imprecise.

I have, however, provided a procedure for assembling the evidence and offering a statistical recommendation regarding a faculty member's course evaluations. Ultimately, I see the final judgment about teaching effectiveness as a dichotomous choice (for example, acceptable or unacceptable), and hence the statistical tools I recommended are consistent with this judgmental process. But the descriptive and inferential data may be used otherwise.

For example, the confidence interval surrounding a faculty member's combined mean TRF score may help clarify a faculty member's teaching performance post hoc if it becomes important to know more than whether an absolute or relative standard of performance has been achieved (for example, whether the standard was missed by a tiny amount or a large margin).

Even with unsystematic variability accounted for, Theall in Chapter Five and other analysts are concerned with the distinction between faculty who "miss by an inch" and those who "miss by a mile." But the visual display and supplemental statistical tests can answer these questions. Is the faculty member better than the lowest 20 percent? The lowest 30 percent? The lowest 40 percent? And as I mentioned previously, the calculation of an effect size may tell us not only whether a difference is statistically significant but also the magnitude of that difference.

In conclusion, I repeat my thanks to Mike Theall and colleagues for commenting on my suggestions for improving the judgments about teaching effectiveness using TRFs. I hope that this dialogue has emboldened some to consider giving my suggestions a try and others to continue the search for better evaluation techniques.

References

d'Apollonia, S., Lou, Y., and Abrami, P. C. "Making the Grade: A Meta-Analysis on the Influence of Grade Inflation on Student Ratings." Paper presented at the 79th Annual Meeting of the American Educational Research Association, San Diego, Apr. 1998.
Greenwald, A. G., and Gillmore, G. M. "Grading Leniency Is a Removable Contaminant of Student Ratings." *American Psychologist*, 1997, 52, 1209–1217.

PHILIP C. ABRAMI *is professor and director of the Centre for the Study of Learning and Performance at Concordia University, Montreal, Quebec, Canada.*

INDEX

Abrami, P. C., 3, 6, 18, 20, 30, 36, 47, 51, 59, 64, 65, 66, 67, 68, 69, 71, 77, 87, 89, 90, 91, 94, 95, 97, 98, 102
Academic Freedom and Tenure Committee (CAUT), 65
ACH scores, 65, 79
AERA Special Interest Group, 89
Aleamoni, L. M., 48, 71, 92, 94
Alumni ratings: as instructional effectiveness indicator, 2; validity of, 11
Ambady, N., 16, 18, 19, 23
American Psychological Association (APA), 4, 27
Arreola, R. A., 48, 51, 52, 92, 93, 94
Assessment-criterion relationships, 35

Ballantyne, C., 33
Bandura, A., 47
Batista, E. E., 31, 37
Blackburn, R. T., 36
Board of Educational Affairs (APA), 4
Body language measurement, 18–19
Boice, R., 47
Brandenburg, G. C., 9, 31, 37
Braskamp, L. A., 13, 31, 36, 41

Canadian Association of University Teachers (CAUT), 64, 65
Cashin, P. A., 71, 92–93
CAUT report (1973), 65
Ceci, S. J., 16, 21, 22, 23, 47, 64, 66, 67
Centra, J. A., 32, 33, 34, 36, 49, 50, 52, 93
Change magazine, 47
Chronicle of Higher Education, 45, 49, 93
Clark, M. J., 36
Classic measurement theory, 78
Cognitive/metacognitive factors, 4
Cohen, J., 12, 13, 14
Cohen, P. A., 12, 15, 16, 17, 30, 36, 46, 48, 49, 50, 65, 93, 95
Consequential validity aspects: collecting evidence based on, 37–40; described, 29
"Construct validation approach," 11
Construct validity: aspects of, 28–29; threats to, 29–30
Content validity aspects: collecting evidence based on, 32–33; described, 29
Conway, C. G., 31

Cornell University, 21
Costin, F., 12, 31, 37
Criterion-referenced evaluation: norm-referenced vs., 71; statistical procedures for, 75–76; testing procedures for, 75; TRF scores combined in, 76–77; visual displays of criterion data for, 77
Cronbach, L. J., 27
Crumbley, L., 64

Damron, J. C., 64
d'Apollonia, S., 20, 30, 36, 51, 64, 65, 66, 68, 69, 77, 95, 98
Developmental Psychology course (Cornell University), 21
Developmental/social factors, 5
Dickens, W. J., 48, 67
Distinguished (Elderly) Teacher Awards, 11
Donnelly, F. A., 16, 17, 23, 47, 66
Doyle, K. O., 16, 17, 32
"Dr. Fox effect," 17
"Dr. Fox study," 17–18, 23, 24, 47, 66
Dwinell, P. L., 33

Evaluation practice: basic considerations for good, 51–54; norm-referenced vs. criterion-referenced, 71; recommended guidelines for, 3. *See also* Student ratings
External validity aspects: collecting evidence based on, 35–36; described, 29

Faculty: avoiding undermining rating process, 41; learning from highly rated, 12–13; "professorial melancholia" suffered by, 47; ratings based on popularity of, 49; student qualification to rate, 48–49; student qualification and gender of, 50; TRFs to measure impact on learning by, 65–66. *See also* Teaching effectiveness
Feldman, K. A., 12, 14, 15, 19, 31, 33, 34, 37, 50, 65, 91, 94
Fleiner, H., 15
Franklin, J. L., 2, 3, 45, 46, 48, 50, 51, 52, 56, 90, 91, 93, 94
Frey, P. W., 18, 49

Gaubatz, N. B., 50
Generalizability validity aspects: collecting evidence based on, 36–37; described, 29

Back Issue/Subscription Order Form

Copy or detach and send to:
Jossey-Bass Publishers, 350 Sansome Street, San Francisco CA 94104-1342

Call or fax toll free!
Phone 888-378-2537 6AM-5PM PST; Fax 800-605-2665

Back issues: Please send me the following issues at $24 each:
(Important: please include series initials and issue number, such as IR90)

1. IR _____

_____

_____

$ _____ Total for single issues

$ _____ Shipping charges (for single issues **only;** subscriptions are exempt from shipping charges): Up to $30, add $5^{50} • $30^{01}–$50, add $6^{50} $50^{01}–$75, add $8 • $75^{01}–$100, add $10, $100^{01}–$150, add $12 Over $150, call for shipping charge

Subscriptions Please ❏ start ❏ renew my subscription to *New Directions for Institutional Research* for the year _____ at the following rate:

U.S. ❏ Individual $59 ❏ Institutional $109
Canada: ❏ Individual $59 ❏ Institutional $154
All Others: ❏ Individual $83 ❏ Institutional $183

NOTE: Subscriptions are quarterly, and are for the calendar year only. Subscriptions begin with the Spring issue of the year indicated above.

$ _____ Total single issues and subscriptions (Add appropriate sales tax for your state for single issue orders. No sales tax for U.S. subscriptions. Canadian residents, add GST for subscriptions and single issues.)

❏ Payment enclosed (U.S. check or money order only)
❏ VISA, MC, AmEx, Discover Card #_____ Exp. date_____

Signature _____ Day phone _____
❏ Bill me (U.S. institutional orders only. Purchase order required)
Purchase order #_____
Federal Tax ID 135593032 GST 89102-8052

Name _____
Address _____

_____

Phone_____ E-mail _____

For more information about Jossey-Bass Publishers, visit our Web site at:
www.josseybass.com **PRIORITY CODE = ND1**